THE NATIONAL CURRICULUM

To the staff of the Education Department at Keele University and the teachers of Staffordshire and Shropshire for their commitment to their important work

The National Curriculum:

A Study in Policy

Edited by

Michael Barber

KEELEUNIVERSITY**PRESS**

First published in 1996 by
Keele University Press
Keele, Staffordshire

© Respective contributors

Composed by KUP
Printed on acid-free paper
by Hartnolls, Bodmin,
Cornwall, England

ISBN 1 85331 115 4

Contents

List of Abbreviations   6

Introduction   7

1. The Roots of Controversy   9
    Michael Barber

2. The National Curriculum Controversy   33
    Michael Barber

3. The National Curriculum and its Assessment   74
    Chris Woodhead

4. The National Curriculum and the Policy Process   88
    Sheila Dainton

Bibliography   121

Appendix I: Interim Dearing Report, July 1993   125

Appendix II: Final Dearing Report, December 1993   132

Index   139

Abbreviations

AMMA Assistant Masters' and Mistresses' Association, now ATL
ATL Association of Teachers and Lecturers
CPS Centre for Policy Studies
DES Department of Education and Science, now **DFEE**
DFE Department for Education, now **DFEE**, Department for Education and Employment
DTI Department of Trade and Industry
ERA Education Reform Act
FEFC Further Education Funding Council
GMS Grant Maintained Schools
GNVQ General National Vocational Qualifications
ILEA Inner London Education Authority
HEFC Higher Education Funding Council
HMCI Her Majesty's Chief Inspector
HMI Her Majesty's Inspectors
LMS Local Management of Schools
MSC Manpower Services Commission
NAHT National Association of Head Teachers
NASUWT National Association of Schoolmasters and Union of Women Teachers

NATFHE National Association of Teachers in Further and Higher Education
NCC National Curriculum Council
NCVQ National Council for Vocational Qualifications
NUT National Union of Teachers
OFSTED Office for Standards in Education
ROTT Record of Teacher Time
SCAA School Curriculum and Assessment Authority
SCDC School Curriculum and Development Committee
SEC Secondary Examination Council
SEAC School Examination and Assessment Council
STRB School Teachers' Review Body
TES *Times Educational Supplement*
TGAT Task Group on Assessment and Testing
THES *Times Higher Educational Supplement*
TVEI Technical and Vocational Education Initiative

Introduction

This book is intended to provide a concise overview of the policy conflict over the National Curriculum. It is in four chapters. The first examines the historical background to and origins of the National Curriculum controversy. The second examines the controversy itself. These chapters are intended to provide both an entertaining narrative and a substantial degree of analysis of the policy process. In particular, some of the vital speeches and texts on the National Curriculum are examined in depth.

The third and fourth chapters provide views from two of the most important protagonists in the controversy. In Chapter Three Chris Woodhead (who was Deputy Chief Executive, then Chief Executive of the National Curriculum Council before becoming Chief Executive of the School Curriculum and Assessment Authority) sets out robustly the case for the National Curriculum and, in his famously trenchant style, takes on its critics.

In Chapter Four, Sheila Dainton, an Assistant Secretary at the Association of Teachers and Lecturers (ATL), sets out the view from a professional association. Throughout the debates of the early 1990s Sheila Dainton was one of the most constructive and effective critics of government curriculum policy and through her and others, the ATL played a major part in bringing about the Dearing settlement.

The recommendations of the two Dearing Reports, which set out the ground rules for the National Curriculum for the rest of this century, are included in the appendices.

There have been a number of specifically Welsh aspects to the curriculum controversy and I should make clear at the outset that these are not dealt with in this book. This does not imply that they are unimportant: on the contrary, they are worth a book on their own, but not one written by me!

It has been both fascinating and rewarding to explore one of the pre-eminent educational controversies of the twentieth century. Of course, the dust has barely settled and many of the judgements must therefore be considered provisional. In the chapters I have written I have chosen to make judgements and take the risk of being proved wrong rather than to err on the side of caution. I hope this makes the book a more provocative read.

There are many people to whom I should offer thanks. Staff and many members of the National Union of Teachers (NUT), who employed me during these years until 1993, were unfailingly supportive of my work and indeed some of the judgements I reach are based on their wisdom and insight. Of course, I take full responsibility for the judgements reached here and any errors made. Though I have on occasions since leaving the NUT reached different conclusions about some important curriculum and assessment issues, I do not underestimate the skill and insight with which the Union has promoted its case.

I am also grateful to the support and friendships of many colleagues in Keele. I hope the modest contribution this book will make to the Keele Centre for Educational Policy Studies will help to repay that debt.

Michael Barber

Notes on Contributors

Michael Barber is Professor of Education at the Institute of Education, London University. He was Head of the Education and Equal Opportunities Department at the NUT from 1989 to 1993 and Professor of Education at Keele University from 1993 to 1995.

Chris Woodhead is Her Majesty's Chief Inspector of Schools. He was Chief Executive of the National Curriculum Council and then of the School Curriculum and Assessment Authority.

Sheila Dainton is an Assistant Secretary in the Policy Unit of the Association of Teachers and Lecturers (ATL). From 1988 she represented ATL on the National Curriculum Council/Teachers' Associations Group, and from 1993 on the School Curriculum and Assessment Authority/ Teachers' Associations Group.

1
The Roots of Controversy

Michael Barber

Introduction

The controversy over the National Curriculum, which has been one of the dominant themes of the last decade of educational politics, involves a series of interlocking issues. Once a government decides to legislate for a curriculum, it raises complex questions: What should the curriculum consist of? What should its intellectual basis be? How should those decisions be reached? How do decisions about the curriculum relate to decisions about educational policy in general? And how do all these issues relate to the traditions of education and the wider culture of the country in question?

This opening chapter is designed to examine these important questions as a prelude to an examination, in the next chapter, of the National Curriculum controversy itself. The first section of this chapter looks at possible models of the curriculum which will enable us in the next chapter to judge the National Curriculum against some criteria provided by curriculum theory. The second section examines the historical origins of the National Curriculum controversy. It sketches in outline the story of curriculum decision-making in England and Wales since the Newcastle Commission of 1863. It consciously examines the historical record as an attempt to explain the present rather than to give a self-contained historical account. The third section looks at the National Curriculum proposals in the context of the government's wider reform agenda. The chapter concludes with an examination of Margaret Thatcher's speech to the Conservative Party Conference in 1987. The intention is that by the end of this chapter the reader will be able to understand in context the controversy described in the next chapter. The chapter is also intended to provide an insight into the policy process in education in general.

Models of the curriculum

There is an extensive literature in curriculum theory. In a brief book such as this it is impossible to do justice to the many significant theorists who have turned their minds to the complex issues of what the curriculum does or should consist of and how its content should be determined. The intention here is to draw attention to some of the main traditions in this thinking. This demands, in the first place, a definition of the curriculum. The debate about this alone runs to many volumes. It raises issues such as whether the curriculum is what is taught or what is learnt (two clearly different things) and whether the curriculum includes all that is taught (or learnt) or merely the planned formal courses of study. This, in turn, raises the question of the hidden curriculum and, indeed, the question of intent. Behind the formal planned curriculum of schools, is there a hidden agenda related, for example, to establishing respect for authority, the maintenance of class divisions, or passive acceptance of the social *status quo*? Or are there schools whose underlying agenda is to ferment discontent with society as it is, or even to promote social revolution?

Each of these issues will rise to the surface from time to time as we examine the ebb and flow of the National Curriculum controversy. What matters at this point is to establish a working definition that will enable us to re-examine the various curriculum traditions. In my view the best such definition is that provided by Mike Golby (in Moon *et al.*, 1989). There he suggests that: 'The curriculum is what school is for. Whatever other functions and purposes the school may serve, what it sets out to teach and what it does teach lies at the heart of its existence.' He also points out that understanding of curriculum is deficient in this country: 'for the curriculum of schools has been generally taken for granted, its structure and rationale unexamined outside the ranks of the education professionals'. The lack of debate outside this charmed circle in part explains why the government was able, in the late 1980s, to impose a national curriculum which had no explicit rationale at all. The absence of a national curriculum in the postwar era may help to explain why the curriculum was assumed to be an issue only for the profession. To explain its implicit rationale it is necessary to examine some of the predominant traditions in curriculum theory.

The liberal-humanist tradition

Perhaps the most important approach over the last century and a half has been the liberal-humanist tradition. Exponents of this view of the curriculum would argue that during two millennia western thought has developed a sophisticated understanding of people and the universe which they inhabit. This understanding is divided into a series of disciplines, such as science and philosophy, which examine specific aspects of human experience and which have developed their own traditions and approaches to explaining the world and arriving at the true, the good and the beautiful, or the nearest possible approximation. The aim of the school curriculum, in the liberal-humanist view, is to introduce pupils to each form of thought or 'community of discourse'. The result is likely to be a knowledge centred curriculum based on subjects. Historically, this view of the curriculum has had a powerful influence, especially in the independent and grammar school sectors.

It has been subjected to three broad lines of attack. Firstly, it has been argued that a liberal-humanist approach is ill-suited to the needs of the less able. This was the argument, for example, of the Norwood Report, published in 1943. It proposed a broadly liberal-humanist curriculum approach for 'the pupil who is interested in learning for its own sake, who can grasp an argument or follow a piece of connected reason ...', but it also suggests there are two other types of pupils: one 'whose interests and abilities lie markedly in the field of applied science or applied art' for whom a technical curriculum would be appropriate; the other would be for those who deal 'more easily with concrete things than with ideas. He may have much ability, but it will be in the realm of facts' (Norwood Report, pp. 2–3). Thus, the assumption of Norwood and many who came later was that the liberal-humanist tradition was only suitable for the more able grammar school type. The Dearing Report's concern with poor motivation among significant numbers of adolescents is, in part, a distant echo of Norwood.

The second criticism of the liberal-humanist approach is that it is not sufficiently 'relevant' to real life. The philosophical tradition and the study of literature (not to mention the classics) on this argument hardly represent effective preparation for the world of work. Relevance in the modern world demands, among other things, knowledge and understanding of science and technology and a range of work-related skills, which the liberal-humanist tradition fails to provide.

Thirdly, the tradition has been attacked from a progressive point of view. It is, seen from this angle, essentially conservative. Furthermore, it assumes that there is a body of knowledge which must be passed on by teachers to pupils. It is, therefore, the antithesis of progressivism, which is founded on child-centredness.

The progressive tradition

The progressive tradition, by contrast, places the child at the centre of the educational process. In this view, the purpose of education is to unlock the potential of the child. The child will be offered a range of experiences and opportunities through which to discover the world; learning will be an active process of discovery; and the process of learning is considered at least as important if not more so than the product or outcome. The child is learning from his or her direct experience or intuition. In this tradition the curriculum is therefore best viewed as a set of opportunities or experiences, rather than a clearly defined set of knowledge or skills. Teaching becomes a facilitative process and opportunistic in the sense of responding to the needs of individual pupils as they become apparent. Crucial to the whole approach is that the teacher knows the child well. This approach is often associated in its origins with Jean-Jacques Rousseau and John Dewey, though, in the case of Dewey, the association is not entirely accurate.

Progressivism has been attacked vigorously, particularly from the political right in recent years. Its critics argue that it provides no stable common course of study and that it is based on naïve assumptions about children, learning and schools. At its worst, they argue, it provides a lack of discipline, no learning worthy of the name and fails to generate any respect for authority or order.

The tradition has, nevertheless, played an important part in shaping education, particularly primary education, in this country. The Plowden Report (1967) is seen as having initiated a generation of progressivism in primary education. At its best, primary education during this era encouraged enquiring minds, helped promote confidence among children, encouraged effective work in groups and developed children's imaginative powers as well as giving them a solid grounding in the basics. At its worst, it became an unstructured mishmash in which teachers had low expectations and children learnt very little. This was probably most prevalent and most damaging in some schools in heavily urbanized areas. It reached its nadir in the 1970s in the scandal of William Tyndale School in Islington, where a combination of punk progressivism and professional arrogance ensured that pupils received an inadequate education and parents were offended. In the end, the school's downfall contributed to the creation of a climate in which there were demands for schools to be made publicly accountable, the reverberations of which are still with us. Indeed, where progressivism was pushed to extremes, as at William Tyndale, it helped to provoke a backlash which remains an important influence on policy thinking even now. Certainly, the debate about the National Curriculum was laced through with this conflict between progressivism and more traditional approaches. As late as 1995, Chris Woodhead, in his first Annual Lecture as Her Majesty's Chief Inspector, argued that:

What, too often, we have is an emotional commitment to beliefs about the purposes and conduct of education which militates against any genuinely searching educational debate. A commitment, for example, to the belief that education must be relevant to the immediate needs and interests of children; that the teaching of knowledge must be less important than the development of core skills; that the adjective 'didactic' must necessarily have pejorative connotations. (Woodhead, 1995)

His lecture caused considerable fury, suggesting that, whatever the validity of his accusations, the conflict between the progressive and the liberal-humanist traditions is far from over.

The technocratic tradition

A third tradition is the technocratic tradition. This is an approach to curriculum design which assumes that the curriculum can be set down in specific objectives or outcomes. Once these are established it is possible to work backwards from them and to work out how to achieve them. Assessment, in this approach, involves testing whether pupils have achieved the specified objectives. This approach has a powerful appeal for those who plan. It appears tidy, explicit and clear.

There are many recent examples of technocratic influence on the curriculum. The GCSE general and subject criteria are strongly influenced by this approach. However, the best example is the pre-Dearing National Curriculum which set down in great detail, through Programmes of Study, Attainment Targets and Statements of Attainment, what both the content and proposed outcomes of the curriculum at every level should be. The most enduring image of the pre-Dearing National Curriculum – a primary teacher ticking boxes – is a testament to technocracy gone wild.

Of course, it need not be like that. It ought to be possible to specify curriculum outcomes without it becoming a bureaucratic nightmare. It is difficult to describe in clear language a series of learning outcomes, as some of the post-Dearing level descriptors show, but this hardly justifies not attempting it. It seems likely that, as long as we have a national curriculum, an element of the technocratic approach will be with us.

It has, however, been subjected to some important criticisms. One is that it purports to be value-free. In other words, it is an approach to planning a curriculum but it assumes agreement about the goals of the curriculum. Yet in practice these are highly likely to be contested.

Secondly, while some learning objectives can be described, learning is not solely about outcomes, still less about planned outcomes. Most people – if they reflect for a while – can think of important learning experiences which were neither planned nor the objective of the original activity. Learning, to misquote John Lennon, is often what happens while you're making other plans. If this is so, then the narrow view of learning, which underpins the technocratic approach to the curriculum, becomes apparent.

In a sense this is a progressive criticism. A progressive might argue, too, that the technocratic approach assumes, as the liberal-humanist tradition does, that the task of the teacher is to mould the learner. At its most basic this makes the teacher little different from a driving instructor. The liberal-humanist, however, might charge the technocratic approach with failing to give the subject-matter anything more than a subsidiary role, with curriculum content playing second fiddle to the specified learning outcomes. The tension between the technocratic approach and the liberal-humanist tradition is an important theme in the last decade of the National Curriculum debate. Stephen Ball and others have identified a conflict within Conservative educational circles between the cultural-restorationists (adopting the liberal-humanist approach) and industrial-modernizers (taking a more technocratic approach). The tension is revealed in the difference between the Technical and Vocational Education Initiative (TVEI) and the National Curriculum and between the vocational qualifications approved by the National Council for Vocational Qualifications (NCVQ), and GCSE and A-levels approved by the School Curriculum and Assessment Authority (SCAA). It may also help to explain why the National Curriculum in England and Wales is the only one which sets down in detail content (to please the liberal-humanists) and outcomes (to please the technocrats).

The cultural-analysis tradition

The final tradition to be identified here is the cultural-analysis tradition. This is probably most effectively described in Denis Lawton's work, though its origins go much further back. In this view the chief task of schools is to transmit elements of a culture from one generation to the next. The curriculum, to use Mike Golby's words (Moon et al., 1989), is seen as a cultural artefact which emerges from a social negotiation between generations. Though Dewey tends to be lumped into the progressive camp, he described this cultural-analysis tradition very well:

> ... the first office of the social organ we call the school is to provide a simplified environment. It selects the features which are fairly fundamental and capable of being responded to by the young. Then it establishes a progressive order, using the factors first acquired as a means of gaining insight into what is more complicated ... it is the business of the school environment to eliminate so far as possible the unworthy features of the existing environment from influence upon mental habitudes ... As a society becomes more enlightened, it realises that it is responsible not to transmit and conserve the whole of its existing achievements, but only such as make for a better future society. The school is the chief agency for the accomplishment of this end. (Dewey, 1916, p. 20)

This is an attractive image of the school curriculum and one that is likely to have wide appeal. That does not mean it is beyond criticism. Both Dewey's and Golby's descriptions gloss over the crunch question of precisely who will decide the content of the curriculum. Is it a job for government, teachers or parents? Who represents the generations in the social negotiation? How will the decisions be made? Will the curriculum in practice reflect the views of a particular class or group within society? Even if we agreed with the idea of a social negotiation, involving all the relevant interests, the tough 'power' questions remain. Anyone who participated in the ten years of debate over the National Curriculum knows that any negotiation over its shape or content is likely to be controversial. Consensus sounds attractive but may, in practice, be a chimera. The other question-mark over the cultural-analysis tradition is whether it is appropriate for an era of very rapid, social, economic, technological and, therefore, cultural change. It is surely conceivable that the social negotiation would end up agreeing yesterday's curriculum for children destined to live in tomorrow's world. Indeed, the present National Curriculum might be flawed in precisely this respect.

The origins of the National Curriculum

On the day that R. A. Butler was appointed President of the Board of Education in 1941, he had a conversation with Winston Churchill which has become justly famous (see Butler, 1971). They talked for a while about evacuating children from the cities to spare them from the Blitz. Then, changing the subject with that combination of imperiousness and mischief for which Churchill was well known, the Prime Minister said: 'I should be grateful if you could introduce a note of patriotism into the schools ... Tell the children that Wolfe won Quebec.' Butler hesitated. This sounded very much like an instruction from the Prime Minister for the government to impose a curriculum, which was not the sort of thing British governments did. Churchill then put him out of his misery: 'I don't mean by instruction,' he explained, 'but by example.' This appears to have been the only conversation the two ever had about the curriculum. It was certainly the nearest that the most interventionist government of the twentieth century ever came even to considering a national curriculum. A government which did not hesitate to fix the price of hake daily was reluctant to prescribe even a single element of curriculum content.

There were two broad reasons for this reluctance. One was that in the 1920s the government had arrived at an unofficial compromise with the teaching profession. In the late nineteenth century the government had had no qualms about imposing a curriculum on the elementary schools. The system of payment by results, which ruled in the elementary sector from 1870 to the mid-1890s, set down through an annually revised code what elementary teachers should teach and how it should be tested. The schools' grants and hence teachers' pay depended on the outcome. The purpose of the elementary schools, as far as the ruling classes were concerned, was to provide the mass of the population with the necessary grounding in the three Rs and ensure that they imbibed a heavy dose of Victorian morality. The same imposition did not, of course, apply to the public schools which the sons, and some of the daughters, of the ruling élite attended. The elementary teachers, through the National Union of Teachers (NUT), fiercely resisted payment by results and, after a generation, succeeded in removing its iniquities from the scene. Over the next twenty to thirty years a new settlement was reached. By the early 1920s the government's greatest anxiety was that teachers and their unions would become an integral part of the newly assertive Labour movement. They had good grounds for such anxiety. The revolutions in Russia and Germany at the end of the First World War had included large numbers of teachers among their leaders. In 1919 the NUT had a referendum in which a significant minority voted in favour of affiliation with the Labour Party. The compromise proposed by the government to avoid this most dreadful of outcomes was that teachers would be incorporated to some extent as partners in the policy process and control over the curriculum would largely be ceded to them. This new-found level of influence and respectability would, government ministers in the early 1920s correctly surmised, be sufficient to detach teachers from the rest of the labour movement. Whether any of this passed through Butler's incisive mind as he stood in Churchill's office that day in 1941 is difficult to say. By then the compromise of the early 1920s seemed to be the natural order of things. The tensions in the 1930s had been to do with resourcing, or rather lack of it, not the curriculum.

The second reason why Churchill and Butler baulked at prescribing the curriculum was much more straightforward. The country was at war to save democracy from fascism. At the time it was generally believed that prescribing the curriculum was something that fascists did and democrats did not. A fascinating insight into this point is provided by a debate over an obscure amendment which was put and defeated during the committee stage of Butler's 1944 Education Bill. I described it thus in my book on the 1944 Education Act:

> Lieutenant-Colonel Sir Thomas Moore, MP for Ayr Burghs, moved that there should be included in the section on adult education, 'part time education for all male persons in the duties and obligations of citizenship and in the elementary functions of the Armed Forces of the Crown', and 'part time education for all female persons in homecraft, motherhood and the responsibilities of citizenship'. His amendment reflected strongly held views among some back-bench Conservative MPs; it posed little threat to Butler, however, since to introduce such a major new element of policy at the report stage was frowned upon.
>
> Lt.-Col. Moore acknowledged this by apologizing at the outset. He soon became further embarrassed because Rear-Admiral Beamish who had planned to support him failed to turn up. He argued that:

> The future of our country depends upon whether our youth accepts
> its full responsibility towards its neighbour, its family and the state.
> The Armed Forces … are a means … of teaching adolescents self-
> discipline, reliability and honesty … As regards our girls, I think
> every father and mother would admit that they and their children
> would have been very much better had they been taught homecraft
> and motherhood. (Hansard, 9 May 1944)

At this point, much of the House dissolved into laughter. It was the
nearest the debates on the Bill came to sexual innuendo.

> Butler intervened, hoping to minimise the embarrassment of his
> lobby fodder: 'Does my hon. and gallant friend mean mothercraft?' But
> Lt.-Col. Moore meant 'mothercraft and motherhood', he asserted: 'I
> am certain the future of our race, mixed though it be, would be far
> sounder' if local authorities were required to ensure that these sub-
> jects were taught.

> Moore found little support. The MP for Liverpool (Scotland Divi-
> sion), Mr Logan, felt that 'It would be better to keep girls off the streets
> at night, have a curfew for them and for their mothers and fathers as
> well, so that they would all be in their homes at a proper time each
> night.'

> W. G. Cove, the sharp and witty Labour MP, and spokesperson for
> the NUT, took a more serious view of Moore's proposals: 'In his tone
> and attitude, and in some of the expressions he used, I thought he was
> very near Hitler.' (Barber, 1994, pp. 98–9)

The 1944 Education Act itself, the seminal document of mid-twentieth-
century education, included no curriculum requirements at all. Even its
paragraph of broad principle interestingly avoids any implication of national curriculum specification. The difference between the 1944 text and
its 1988 echo is instructive: '… it shall be the duty of the local education
authority for every area, so far as their powers extend, to contribute
towards the spiritual, moral, mental and physical development of the
community …' (1944 Education Act, Section 7). The 1988 text, by contrast, proposes a curriculum which is balanced and broadly based and
which:

> (a) promotes the spiritual, moral, cultural, mental and physical devel-
> opment of pupils at the school and of society; and (b) prepares such
> pupils for the opportunities, responsibilities and experiences of adult
> life. (1988 Education Act, Section 1)

The mid-century association of curriculum prescription with fascism exerted a powerful influence on postwar educational thinking. Indeed, within the teaching profession the view that state intervention in the curriculum was dangerous, became a shibboleth. Ronald Gould, the General Secretary of the NUT from the mid-1940s until 1970 and the most influential of all postwar teacher leaders, put it like this: 'I have heard it said that the existence in this country of 146 strong, vigorous LEAs safeguards democracy and lessens the risk of dictatorship ... an even greater safeguard is the existence of a quarter of a million teachers who are free to decide what should be taught and how it should be taught' (quoted in Barber, 1992, p. 35). Gould put this argument to practical effect in the early 1960s when, for the first time in the postwar era, central government attempted to dip its toe in the murky waters of the curriculum. The then Conservative government proposed the establishment of a curriculum study group within the Department of Education and Science. From the perspective of the 1990s this seems innocuous enough, but at the time it provoked a storm. Gould and many of his colleagues in the profession argued that this was the beginning of the slippery slope to fascism.

Out of the ensuing row emerged the Schools' Council. To prevent the dangers that Gould had warned against, it was a body based on the policy partnership of central government, local government and teachers and, significantly, its constitution in the early days specified that the Council and its committees must have a majority of teachers among their members. For the best part of two decades the Schools' Council headed off significant curriculum intervention from central government. It advanced a wide range of significant national curriculum developments, such as the Schools' Council History Project. More importantly, it had an underlying philosophy based on Jean Ruddock's aphorism that there should be: 'No curriculum development without teacher development' (quoted in Plaskow, 1985).

Its underlying assumption was consistent with Gould's beliefs. Teachers would maintain control over the curriculum which, in turn, would be achieved and developed by encouraging teachers to experiment. Their developments would then be disseminated and adopted, or not, by other members of the profession. This led to some substantial achievements. However, partly because of its philosophical stance, it failed to bring about national consensus either on the scope and content of the overall curriculum, or on much needed reform of the public examination system.

Until the mid-1970s this failure did not matter much. Then came the economic crisis. We tend to remember the 1973 oil crisis for contributing to a miners' strike, a 3-day week and the fall of a Heath government, but in the longer run its impact was much more severe. The weakness of the British economy was exposed; public expenditure was put under pressure. For education, this had two direct consequences. Firstly, it led politicians to scrutinize more carefully the extent to which the money they were investing in education was being spent wisely. Secondly, they sought explanations for, and solutions to, the nation's economic problems.Both, as night follows day, led them to question the purposes of education and the extent to which society was being well served by its schools. From that moment on it was inevitable that the curriculum would become, once again, a political issue.

Another factor hugely affected the politicians' interest in the school curriculum in the mid-1970s. For some years, in the Black Papers, a number of influential right-wing polemicists had attacked the insidious influence – as they saw it – of teachers over what went on in schools. Following the comprehensive reforms of the mid-1960s and, in the aftermath of the Plowden Report, the growing adherence to child-centred approaches in primary schools, there was an educational crisis brewing, claimed the Black Paperites, in which excellence would be undermined, standards would fall and a woolly liberal relativism would rule. Neither the 1970–4 Heath government nor its Labour successor in its first year was troubled or unduly influenced by this line of attack. All was changed, however, by the crackpot antics at William Tyndale Junior School in 1975. There, a handful of teachers took child-centredness and professional control of the curriculum to an extreme. Over a series of months, they defied their governors and their local authority, the Inner London Education authority (ILEA), and provided the popular press with a series of headlines. Public concern reached such a pitch that the politicians, particularly a Labour government fighting for its life because of its slender majority, were bound to react. The teachers at William Tyndale probably did more than any other group of individuals to give widespread credence to the Black Paper philosophy and to ensure that professional accountability and hence curriculum prescription became a significant part of the educational agenda.

The immediate political response came from the ILEA, which established an inquiry under Robin Auld. This is one of the great postwar texts on the issues of accountability and professionalism. The following extracts will suffice to provide an insight, both into the appalling state of affairs inside William Tyndale Junior School and to the absence of accountability mechanisms, which, from the perspective of the 1990s, seem almost incredible:

Mr Ellis [the headteacher] said that he did not give a damn about parents, Managers or anybody else, that teachers were 'the pros at the game', and that nobody else had any right to judge them. Mrs Burnett pointed out that, although parents were not 'pros' in the field of education, they could recognize if their children were happy and interested in school, and that teachers could not ride roughshod over parents' feelings. In the course of the discussion that followed Mrs Burnett was horrified to hear Mr Ellis describe parents as either 'working class fascists or middle class trendies out for their own children'. (Auld Report, para 514)

[The LEA had] no policy:
1. as to standards of attainment at which primary schools should aim;
2. as to the aims and objectives of the primary education being pro-
    vided in its schools ...;
3. as to the methods of teaching to be adopted in its schools.
    (Auld Report)

The economic crisis of the mid-1970s and the William Tyndale affair provide the context for the now famous speech by the then Prime Minister, James Callaghan, at Ruskin College on 18 October 1976. The speech is often referred to as the beginning of the debate about accountability, a debate which culminated in the National Curriculum. It is rarely seen in its context and hardly ever quoted at length. In fact, the speech bears much closer analysis than it normally receives. After referring to Ruskin College's heritage and its close association with the trade-union movement, Callaghan addressed his main theme:

> ... higher standards than in the past are also required in the general educational field. It is not enough to say that standards in this field have or have not declined. With the increasing complexity of modern life we cannot be satisfied with maintaining existing standards, let alone observe any decline. We must aim for something better.

The speech had been widely trailed and Callaghan knew he was walking into a storm:

> There have been one or two ripples of interest in the education world in anticipation of this visit. I hope the publicity will do Ruskin College some good and I don't think it will do the world of education any harm. I must thank all those who have inundated me with advice, some helpful, and others telling me less politely to keep off the grass ... It is almost as though some people would wish that the subject matter should not have public attention focused on it; nor that profane hands should be allowed to touch it.

With this rebuke to some leaders of the teaching profession behind him, he took the argument a stage further:

> I cannot believe that this is a considered reaction. The Labour move-ment has always cherished education: free education, comprehensive education, adult education, education for life. There is nothing wrong with non-educationalists, even a Prime Minister, talking about it now

and again. Everyone is allowed to put his oar in on how to overcome our economic problems ... Very important too. But, I venture to say, not as important in the long run as preparing future generations for life. R. H. Tawney ... wrote that the endowment of children is the most precious of the natural resources of the community. So I do not hesitate to discuss how those endowments should be nurtured.

Then he drove his argument home:

I take it that no one claims exclusive rights in this field. We spend £6 billion a year on education, so there will be discussion. But let it be national. If everything is reduced to such phrases as 'educational freedom versus state control' we shall get nowhere.

Gould's argument, quoted above, is thus dismissed. Then, a more conciliatory tone:

I repeat that parents, teachers, learned and professional bodies, representatives of higher education and both sides of industry, together with Government, all have an important part to play in formulating and expressing the purpose of education and the standards that we need.

Callaghan then outlined his substantive criticisms:

First let me say, so that there should be no misunderstanding, that I have been very impressed in the schools I have visited by the enthusiasm and dedication of the teaching profession, by the variety of courses that are offered in our comprehensive schools, especially in arts and crafts as well as in other subjects; and by the alertness and keenness of many of the pupils. Clearly, life at school is far more full and creative than it was many years ago. I would also like to thank the children who have been kind enough to write to me after I visited their schools: and well-written letters they were. I recognise that teachers occupy a special place in these discussions because of their real sense of professionalism and vocation about their work. But I am concerned on my journeys to find complaints from industry that new recruits from the schools sometimes do not have the basic tools to do the job that is required.

I have been concerned to find that many of our best trained students who have completed the higher levels of education at university or polytechnic have no desire to join industry. Their preferences are to stay in academic life or to find their way into the Civil Service. There seems to be a need for a more technological bias in science teaching that will lead towards practical applications in industry rather than towards academic studies. Or, to take other examples, why is it that such a high proportion of girls abandon science before leaving school? Then there is concern about the standards of numeracy of school-leavers. Is there not a case for a professional review of the mathematics needed by industry at different levels? To what extent are these deficiencies the result of insufficient coordination between schools and industry? Indeed how much of the criticism about basic skills and attitudes is due to industry's own shortcomings rather than to the educational system? Why is it that 30,000 vacancies for students in science and engineering in our universities were not taken up last year while the humanities courses were full? On another aspect there is the unease felt by parents and others about the new informal methods of teaching which seem to produce excellent results when they are in well-qualified hands but are much more dubious when they are not. They seem to be best accepted where strong parent–teacher links exist. There is little wrong with the range and diversity of our courses. But is there sufficient thoroughness and depth in those required in after life to make a living?

In this last paragraph the shadow of the William Tyndale controversy is plain. Callaghan was too shrewd a politician not to see that his critics in the profession would try to paint him with a Black Paper brush. He preferred to get his retaliation in first:

> These are proper subjects for discussion and debate. And it should be a rational debate based on the facts. My remarks are not a clarion call to Black Paper prejudices. We all know those who claim to defend standards but who in reality are simply seeking to defend old privilege and inequalities. It is not my intention to become enmeshed in such problems as whether there should be a basic curriculum with universal standards although I am inclined to think that there should be – nor about such other issues on which there is a divided professional opinion … What I am saying is that where there is legitimate public concern it will be to the advantage of all involved in the education field if these concerns are aired and shortcomings righted or fears put to rest.

As he did elsewhere in the speech, Callaghan at this point attempted to find a middle way between the teaching profession and its critics. In this, as in other respects, he differed markedly from his Tory successors a decade later: 'To the critics I would say that we must carry the teaching profession with us. They have the expertise and the professional approach. To the teachers I would say that you must satisfy the parents and industry that what you are doing meets their requirements and the needs of our children …' The prophetic nature of his next remark deserves careful attention. It highlights the extent to which the next decade was one of inadequate response from the teaching profession, even though the writing was on the wall: 'For if the public is not convinced then the profession will be laying up trouble for itself in the future.'

Having raised, however equivocally, the issue of a basic curriculum and universal standards, Callaghan went on to outline what its scope and character might be:

The goals of our education, from nursery school through to adult education, are clear enough. They are to equip children to the best of their ability for a lively, constructive place in society and also to fit them to do a job of work. Not one or the other, but both. For many years the accent was simply on fitting a so-called inferior group of children with just enough learning to earn their living in the factory. Labour has attacked that attitude consistently, during 60 or 70 years and throughout my childhood. There is now widespread recognition of the need to cater for a child's personality, to let it flower in the fullest possible way.

The balance was wrong in the past. We have a responsibility now to see that we do not get it wrong in the other direction. There is no virtue in producing socially well-adjusted members of society who are unemployed because they do not have the skills. Nor at the other extreme must they be technically efficient robots. Both of the basic purposes of education require the same essential tools. These are basic literacy, basic numeracy, the understanding of how to live and work together, respect for others, respect for the individual.

This means acquiring certain basic knowledge, and skills and reasoning ability. It means developing lively inquiring minds and an appetite for further knowledge that will last a lifetime. It means mitigating as far as possible the disadvantages that may be suffered through poor home conditions or physical or mental handicap. Are we aiming in the right direction in these matters?

Again he tried to reassure his professional audience without compromising on his critique:

I do not join those who paint a lurid picture of educational decline because I do not believe it is generally true, although there are examples which give cause for concern. I am raising a further question. It is this. In today's world higher standards are demanded than were required yesterday and there are simply fewer jobs for those without skill. Therefore we demand more from our schools than did our grandparents.

His concerns about the economic state of affairs, which dominated his term of office were now spelt out:

There has been a massive injection of resources into education, mainly to meet increased numbers and partly to raise standards. But in present circumstances there can be little expectation of further increased resources being made available, at any rate for the time being. I fear that those whose only answer to these problems is to call for more money will be disappointed. But that surely cannot be the end of the matter. There is a challenge to us all in these days and a challenge in education is to examine its priorities and to secure as high efficiency as possible by the skilful use of existing resources.

He concluded with an appeal, typical of Labour Prime Ministers, to the traditions of the labour movement: 'It would be a betrayal of [the labour movement's] concern if I did not draw these problems to your attention and put to you specifically some of the responses that will be needed from our educational system' (quoted in Moon *et al.*, 1989, pp. 271–7).

This has been a lengthy examination of Callaghan's speech. It is justified because the speech raised almost all the issues which we have spent the last two decades debating. In that sense, the speech represents the bridge between one era and the next. To my ears at least it seems a model of balance, rational argument and plain speaking, but of course we now know what came later. At the time there was a huge political and professional storm. A combination of this, and the weakness of the government, meant that, in spite of the fact that it had over two years to run, Labour achieved little in relation to the agenda that Callaghan had set.

There were, however, a series of publications on curriculum issues from the Department of Education and Science (DES) and Her Majesty's Inspectors (HMI). In policy terms, these raise an issue which, up to this point, has not been elucidated. For the curriculum story in which we are bound up is also a story of civil servants seeking constantly to increase their influence over the education service.

Before the Second World War the Board of Education, as it was then called, was a relatively weak department, both in relation to the education service and in relation to other departments of state. One minister in the 1930s, with only a touch of exaggeration, dismissed it as 'an outpost of the Treasury'. During the war, the civil servants began to prepare for educational change after the war. They drafted a document which became known as 'The Green Book' (which was, incidentally, the origin of the term Green Paper), setting out their plans for the postwar world. It brought together many of the themes of the education establishment of the time and, like the 1944 Education Act, said little or nothing about the curriculum. What is interesting from our point of view, however, is that the officials who drafted it – working in a hotel in Bournemouth to avoid the Blitz – saw postwar educational reform as an opportunity to increase their own influence. R. S. Wood wrote in a memorandum to his colleagues: '... planning for educational reconstruction provides an admirable opportunity for re-establishing the position of the Board [of Education] as the body competent to lead and to direct the educational system of this country' (quoted in Barber, 1994). And the 1944 Education Act fulfilled these ambitions. Although from our vantage point in the 1990s its centralizing measures appear mild, in its day it was clearly viewed as an Act which strengthened the centre.

The Curriculum Study Group, which Gould and his colleagues saw off in the early 1960s was another attempt by civil servants to increase their influence, this time directly in the curriculum field. Their defeat on this occasion ensured that the department was at best neutral and often hostile to the Schools' Council which was established in place of the Study Group. Over the longer run, however, this proved to be only a temporary setback for the civil servants. Callaghan's speech, and the context in which it was made, provided a new opportunity for the department to strengthen its influence. Hence, the series of publications in which the seeds of a National Curriculum began to take root. The first was a Green Paper entitled 'Education in Schools: A Consultative Document' (cmnd 6869, DES 1977). This explicitly took up the themes of the Great Debate which Callaghan had launched. It followed his lines of criticism and recommended a 'framework for the curriculum' which would include 'a core or protected' element. Further documents in 1978 and 1979 criticized both primary and secondary schools for the lack of balance in the curriculum and for their failure to develop sufficiently planned curricula which took account of the changes in the education service and the wider needs of industry and society. The 1979 HMI Report on 'Aspects of Secondary Education in England' (DES, 1979) suggested that it was necessary 'to think again for a more explicit rationale for the curriculum as a whole'.

The one decisive act of the Labour government was to issue Circular 14/77 (DES, 1977) which asked LEAs about the curriculum in their areas. The responses were published in 1979 and revealed, not surprisingly, substantial variation in curriculum policy across the country. In its report on this exercise, the DES went on to assert that the Secretary of State had a duty to ensure that the work of schools matched national needs. LEAs, it said, ought to have explicit curriculum policies which met national needs, while simultaneously winning local agreement. The report chose once again to urge the establishment of a nationally agreed framework for the curriculum. In the series of reports that followed from the centre, two differing models of a national curriculum emerged: one came from the DES, promoting a subject-based curriculum with an emphasis on the core subjects of English, mathematics and science, while HMI promoted a broader curriculum based not on subjects but on 'areas of experience'.

Meanwhile, the Conservative government that had been elected in 1979 began progressively to weaken and then to undermine the partnership model of decision-making. A government that was so hostile to unions could hardly contemplate with equanimity the existence of a range of national bodies which were, in effect, dominated by the teacher organizations in general and the NUT in particular. In 1983 Sir Keith Joseph announced that the Schools' Council, that quintessential model of partnership, would be abolished. In its place would be the School Curriculum Development Committee (SCDC) and Secondary Examinations Council (SEC): their members would not be representative but appointed by the Secretary of State. The decision outraged the teachers' unions, particularly the NUT. It was further evidence of the growing frustration of politicians and the increasing determination of DES civil servants to extend their influence.

The decision also had an accidental by-product. There was, from that moment on, no national forum in which the professional voice in the curriculum debate could be heard. Alan Evans, then Head of Education at the NUT, sounded out colleagues in other unions and among the LEAs on the possibility of the establishment of a curriculum council of their own, without central government, but he was unable to generate sufficient enthusiasm (Bowe and Ball, 1992). Given the exploitation of this vacuum by central government in the late 1980s, the foresight of Evans's proposal is apparent, but at the time the prevailing view was that sooner or later the *status quo ante* would be restored. With hindsight, of course, it is clear that this was not remotely possible. The forces shifting in favour of both a nationally prescribed curriculum and clearer lines of accountability were too powerful. The White Paper *Better Schools* represented the next step forward in this process. Published in April 1985, *Better Schools* recommended moving towards a nationally agreed curriculum, though it qualified its proposal, arguing that: 'It would not ... be right for the [government's] policy ... to amount to the determination of national syllabuses ...' By comparison with what we now know would follow, this seems mild. At the time it was attacked from within the profession as representing a further step down the dangerous road to government prescription. The NUT's response to *Better Schools*, published later in 1985, makes the point: 'The National Union of Teachers has viewed with concern the attempts made by Government to exert an influence over the curriculum of schools. That concern is heightened when the Union consider the direction in which that influence is being exerted' (NUT, 1985). It went on to suggest that 'the Government's attempt to define the curriculum nationally is misconceived', though it was willing to countenance a broad agreement about aims. The echo of Gould in this response is unmistakable. The problem was, of course, that the threat of fascism had receded into history. Once that had happened, the case for professional control of the curriculum was fatally undermined. Thus, in a public conflict over whether or not there should be a national curriculum the profession was left without a coherent case. Their opposition could therefore easily be portrayed as a self-interested conspiracy against the laity.

At the time, the weakness of the profession's position was not apparent, at least within the profession. Teachers had, after all, been full, and sometimes dominant, partners in the policy process for over half a century.

They had been able to block all previous attempts by central government to gain control over the curriculum, they had achieved the long-standing goal of becoming an all-graduate profession and they still, through the bumpy Burnham process, exerted a powerful influence over pay negotiations and a hold over conditions of service. Though their golden age of influence in the 1950s and '60s had passed, there was still what one might call, perhaps slightly cruelly, a post-imperial glow. In the mid-1980s, however, a combination of factors swept any such notion away. The curriculum in 1985 was, to most teachers' union leaders, a side show. At the top of the agenda were their demands concerning their pay and conditions. The teaching profession found itself in conflict with the Thatcher government on many fronts: curriculum, appraisal, pay, conditions of service and the decision-making process. As the disputes over pay between 1984 and 1986 dragged on, popular support for the unions ebbed.

The government, meanwhile, grew stronger. The miners were defeated. The Westland crisis was overcome. The economy boomed. Kenneth Baker, replacing Keith Joseph, swept away the Burnham machinery and imposed a pay settlement. Then the government won its overwhelming election victory in 1987. For a moment in history it seemed as if the government could do no wrong, while the teaching profession, led by six unions often in conflict with one another, could do little right. A politician who wanted to introduce a national curriculum would be unlikely ever to have a better opportunity than Kenneth Baker had in 1987.

The wider educational project

The National Curriculum proposals formed only one part of a much wider programme of education reform. Though this chapter has sought to keep closely to the theme of the book, the National Curriculum controversy cannot be understood in isolation from the other aspects of reform. While the idea of a national curriculum had been the subject of a decade or more of debate, the same is true, at a less high-profile level, of the idea of applying market principles to public services such as education. It is not the intention in the context of this book to trace the development of those ideas. It is, however, important to understand three issues. Firstly, the ideas on the political right which ultimately informed the 1988 Education Reform Act came not from one strand of Conservative thinking, but from several. Secondly, in the government's view the National Curriculum was important not only for intrinsic reasons, it also had a pivotal place in the wider reform programme. Thirdly, there was a burgeoning conflict between central and local government without which much of the ensuing conflict cannot be understood. Each of these issues is now looked at in turn.

Essentially, three separate but sometimes conflicting strands of Conservative thinking informed the 1988 Education Reform Act. Firstly, there were the cultural-restorationists (Bowe and Ball, 1992) whose aim was, to use a phrase which later came into disrepute, to get back to basics. They believed that a national curriculum should emphasize the three Rs, British history, British literature and the cultural heritage. They railed against the woolly cultural relativism of the 1970s and 1980s. There was an echo in their case of the liberal-humanist tradition, but some of them were so ardent and so shallow in pursuit of these objectives that they were a caricature of a noble curriculum tradition, rather than genuine representatives of it. Indeed, on the fringes some supporters of this line of thinking expressed views which were, in essence, racist.

Secondly, there were the industrial-modernizers. Their argument – drawing on the Callaghan speech among other sources – was that the education service was inadequate to meet the needs of the late twentieth-century British economy. They were keen to see greater emphasis on science and technology, on problem-solving and team work and on universal mastery of the late twentieth-century basics, including information technology. This set of views did not sit altogether easily with those of the cultural-restorationists, and the underlying tension between the groups was reflected in the National Curriculum itself and the controversies that surrounded it. The industrial-modernizers had a number of successes in the mid-1980s, the most notable of which was the Technical and Vocational Education Initiative (TVEI), which began in fourteen pilot LEAs in 1984, ran for a decade and cost over £1 billion during that period – rather more, incidentally, than was invested, even on high estimates, in the National Curriculum. TVEI was the responsibility not of the DES, but of the Manpower Services Commission (MSC), a training and work skills quango under the auspices of the Department of Employment. TVEI and the other MSC initiatives of the mid-1980s therefore represented a threat in bureaucratic terms to the growing influence of the DES. John Major's decision to merge the Education and Employment Departments in the summer of 1995 might finally bring the tensions between the two to an end. The industrial-modernizers also had a small but influential power base, not surprisingly, in the Department of Trade and Industry (DTI), which made significant investment in information technology in schools until Nicholas Ridley, the arch-non-interventionist, became Secretary of State there and pruned what he saw as a fringe activity for the DTI.

The third strand of thinking behind the Conservative education reforms was the idea of the market as the solution to the problems of the public as well as the private sector. Several right-wing pressure groups, pre-eminently the Centre for Policy Studies (CPS), which numbered Margaret Thatcher and Keith Joseph among its founder members, had proposed means of applying market principles to education. In the mid-1980s the favoured option, which Keith Joseph toyed with before rejecting on the advice of DES officials, was vouchers. The idea is relatively simple in conception. The money available for publicly provided education would be given directly to parents in the form of a voucher which they could cash in for a place at any school which had available space. They could, if they chose, also use the voucher as a contribution to the fees of a private school. Officials pointed out that the system would be complex and bureaucratic to administer and would lead to a great increase in the extent to which the state subsidized private education. Where the voucher helped pay for a place in a private school for which a parent was already paying, it would represent, in effect, an addition to public expenditure or a reduction in the resources available for the education of the children of those who, up to that point, had not used private education. Though the idea of the voucher played no part in the 1988 Act, the market philosophy behind it was all important. In relation to the curriculum, the marketeers varied. It was the view of those at the extreme free-market end of the spectrum, a place inhabited by Sheila Lawlor of the CPS among others, that the content of the curriculum should, like everything else, be left to the market. The government, they argued, ought to keep out. This kind of thinking clearly influenced Sir Keith Joseph, who in the Lords in 1988 spoke against Baker's plans for a broad national curriculum.

If these were the three strands of Conservative thinking, how did they mesh together in the 1988 Education Reform Act? The main thrust of the Act was to create an education market. Through the open enrolment, local management of schools and pupil-based funding formulae, schools were put in competition for pupils. A market was created without the need for vouchers. Through the option of grant-maintained status, the local education authority 'monopoly' was broken up. Grant-maintained schools and City Technology Colleges also brought the possibility of greater diversity into the supply side of the market.

The main thrust of the Act was, therefore, to diversify, atomize and divide. The National Curriculum has two roles in this market conception. Firstly, it is the element that unifies, nationalizes and centralizes; it holds the public service together. In Baker's analogy the whole reform was about strengthening the rim and the hub and weakening what was in between (i.e. the LEA). The National Curriculum was a strengthening of the hub. In Stephen Ball's view it was akin to franchising in the private sector. The government was telling schools: 'You run the restaurant, we'll set the menu'. This led him to deride the package as the Kentucky Fried Curriculum.

Secondly, the curriculum and its associated testing requirements would, through the subsequent publication of results, provide parents with information on which to base comparisons between schools and thus, in the government's view, to make an informed market choice. The reforms of 1988 therefore fell short of a full-blown market model. Instead, they created a quasi-market open to powerful regulation from central government. Part of the reason for this was that by 1988 there was a high degree of hostility to local government from central government. This had its origins in attempts by central government to control local government expenditure. From the mid-1970s central government considered that this was necessary as a result of the economic crises of the period, which had led to a need to restrict overall public expenditure. From 1979 onwards the case was reinforced by the ideological hostility of the monetarists at the heart of the Thatcher government to the public sector. In fact, the various tortuous attempts to control local government expenditure failed one after another and led ultimately to the poll tax débâcle. The council tax, introduced to help the government out of the poll tax pit, is effective only because it depends upon central government providing over 80 per cent of all local spending. It turns out to be true that he who pays the piper calls the tune.

The successive attempts of government to contain local expenditure was a powerful cause of the teachers' pay dispute of the mid-1980s which, towards the end, left teachers divided among themselves, local government in turmoil and both in conflict with central government. As if this mix was not potent enough, there were also a series of high profile conflicts between Labour-controlled urban authorities and central government over education and equal opportunity issues. If the most grotesque Labour council, in the days before Kinnock's new realism, was militant-controlled Liverpool, in educational terms some of the decisions in places like Haringey and Brent were not far behind. The headline-grabbing issues tended to emerge from the absurd and shallow implementation of anti-racist or anti-heterosexist policies. Some Labour councils, hung up on the shibboleths of the far left, forgot the need to maintain public consent for their policies and indulged in the worst forms of gesture politics. They concerned themselves with rhetoric rather than substance. They also opened themselves up to attack from the popular press, which gorged itself on a series of 'loony left' stories – some of which were pure journalistic invention – which helped undermine not only the Labour Party, but also local education authorities in general. Since, in many cases, a minority of teachers backed the LEAs, the status of the teaching profession was damaged too. The William Tyndale affair cast a long shadow.

Thatcher explains all

The previous section was a lengthy examination of the educational context in which the National Curriculum and the Education Reform Act were introduced. The next chapter will examine the controversy over Kenneth Baker's National Curriculum proposals and their implementation. This chapter concludes with an examination of a speech by Margaret Thatcher which encapsulates Conservative thinking at the end of the controversies of the early and mid-1980s and at the outset of the new debates which would begin with the 1988 Education Reform Act.

Fresh from her triumph in the summer election of 1987, Margaret

Thatcher received one of her most adulatory receptions when she addressed the Conservative Party conference that autumn. She identified education as the new government's highest priority:

> Our most important task in this Parliament is to raise the quality of education. It's in the national interest and it's in the individual interest of every parent and above all, every child. We want education to be part of the answer to Britain's problems, not part of the cause.
>
> To compete successfully in tomorrow's world – against Japan, Germany and the United States – we need well-educated, well-trained, creative young people. If education is backward today, national performance will be backward tomorrow.

Her opening salvo identifies strongly with the industrial-modernizers' case; she has identified the policy goal. Next she turns to making sure that the blame for the educational weakness she has identified lies not with her government which had already been in power for eight years, but with local government and teachers.

> … it is the plight of individual boys and girls which worries me most. Too often our children don't get the education they need – the education they deserve. And in the inner cities … that opportunity is too often snatched from them by hard-left education authorities and extremist teachers.
>
> Children who need to be able to count and multiply are learning anti-racist mathematics – whatever that may be.
>
> Children who need to be able to express themselves in clear English are being taught political slogans.
>
> Children who need to be taught to respect traditional moral values are being taught that they have an inalienable right to be gay.
>
> Children who need encouragement – and so many children do – are being taught that society offers them no future.
>
> All those children are being cheated of a sound start in life – yes cheated.

There is a powerful element of playing to the gallery here. A packed celebratory Tory conference no doubt enjoyed the sequence of false dichotomies at the heart of the passage. Note too that having picked up the industrial-modernizers' case already, she adds to it a strong dose of cultural-restorationism. On this she builds the case for a no-nonsense back-to-basics national curriculum:

> I believe that government must take primary responsibility for setting standards for the education of our children. That's why we are establishing a national curriculum for basic subjects.
>
> It is vital that all children master essential skills; reading, writing,

spelling, grammar, arithmetic; and that they understand basic science and technology. For good teachers this will provide a foundation on which they can build with their own creative skill and professionalism.

Already in 1987 the seeds of conflict within government circles are apparent. Should the curriculum focus on English, mathematics and science, as the Thatcher speech suggests, or should it be broad and balanced as Kenneth Baker and his DES officials had already proposed? In the context of the 1987 conference speech this scarcely mattered. Having explained the role of a national curriculum in a way that might please both modernizers and traditionalists, Thatcher went on to rally the free-marketeers:

> The Labour left – hard, soft and in-between – hate the idea that people should be able to choose ... The Conservative Party believes in parental choice. We are now about to take two dramatic steps forward in extending choice ... First we will allow popular schools to take in as many children as space permits ... And second we will give parents and governors the right to take their children's school out of the hands of the local authority and into the hands of their own governing body. This will create a new kind of school funded by the state ... These new schools will be independent state schools ... There is no reason at all why local authorities should be a monopoly of free education. What principle suggests this is right? What recent experience or practice suggests is it even sensible? (quoted in Moon *et al.*, 1989, pp. 277–8)

It can be seen from this passage that the Thatcher speech of 1987 weaves together the themes that had emerged to influence Tory education policy in the previous few years. The espousal of a common-sense curriculum, the beliefs in the market and the hostility to local authorities are all plain. Within weeks of this speech Kenneth Baker had introduced what was known at the time as the Great Education Reform Bill. The National Curriculum controversy was about to begin in earnest.

2
The National Curriculum Controversy

Michael Barber

This chapter attempts to explain one of the most bitter and complex controversies in British educational history. It is flawed in at least two ways and it is as well to warn the reader in advance. Firstly, the events described here are so recent that it is not easy to gain sufficient perspective on them. It is important to try to identify the underlying trends of policy and the broad sweep of history. Only eighteen months or so after the second Dearing Report it is not easy to differentiate between aberrations and inevitabilities or between turning points and continuities, since to do so involves making guesses about the future course of events. The second flaw is that I do not write as a detached observer, still less as a disinterested historian, of these events, but as a participant who might be expected, like other participants, to attempt to justify or explain the positions I took up as events unfolded. A degree of bias is inevitable.

The chapter is in five sections. The first deals with the original conception of the National Curriculum at the time of the 1988 Education Reform Act. The second section looks at the professional response to this idea. The third examines the seeds of destruction of the original Baker conception of the National Curriculum. The fourth examines the crisis of 1992–3 which resulted in the test boycott of 1993, and the fifth the Dearing Review of the National Curriculum and its consequences.

The original blueprint

In the last chapter the different strands of opinion on the nature and scope of the National Curriculum were identified. Kenneth Baker, the Secretary of State for Education from 1986 to 1989, the critical period for shaping the original National Curriculum, was very clear where he stood. In his autobiography he nails his colours firmly to the mast in a comment he made on one of his successors, Kenneth Clarke:

> Ken [Clarke] and his ministers had become impatient with the complex detail and prescriptive nature of the curriculum. But the whole purpose of a curriculum is that it sets out in detail the progressive growth in

knowledge which a child has to experience. Vagueness and lack of detail
will allow an inadequate and lazy teacher to skip the important parts.
(Baker, 1993, p. 198)

Baker's determination to insist on a curriculum that was balanced and
broadly based as well as detailed and prescriptive is a good example of an
individual minister making a clear mark on policy. Given Margaret Thatcher's preference for a curriculum focused on the core subjects, a different
Secretary of State – Kenneth Clarke for example – would no doubt have
chosen a different way forward from that chosen by Baker.

Baker's own account of the origins of the National Curriculum is fascinating. It suffers from the faults of many political autobiographies and
cannot be assumed to be entirely accurate. It is, perhaps, more than many,
a work of hagiography as well as autobiography: the author as hero, as it
were. Nevertheless, as a set of insights into the policy process it is essential
reading, and Baker on the whole writes with wit and pace. Interestingly,
he begins his account (in Chapter 9 of his book) with a reference to the
1976 Callaghan speech. He then mentions the 'rambling and inconclu-
sive' discussions which took place during Sir Keith Joseph's tenure.
Implicitly, Baker contrasts this with his own decisive approach:

> I was convinced that the key to raising educational standards across the
> country was a national curriculum … I found that the Department [of
> Education and Science] had spent a lot of time on this subject, but the
> work lacked coherence … I inherited a decision taken just before my
> appointment that an agreement on a national curriculum 'should not
> be thrown away by imposition'. It took me no time at all to discover that
> there was no chance at all of getting a voluntary agreement. The educa-
> tion establishment in university departments of education were deeply
> suspicious, some teachers were determined to fight to death for their
> own subject, while others objected to the whole principle of an imposed
> national curriculum … (Baker, 1993, pp. 189–90)

As a result of these findings, Baker made preparations for a national
curriculum in the first instance behind closed doors and certainly not in
consultation with the profession. It was a way of working which became
endemic, and ultimately contributed to the downfall of Baker's conception. However in the context of 1986–7, with the pay dispute at its height,
his judgement that agreement on this central issue would have been
difficult is probably right. The policy conclusions he drew from this
judgement are more debatable.

In typical fashion Baker first announced his intention to introduce a
national curriculum in a television interview with Matthew Parris on 7
December 1986. According to Baker, Margaret Thatcher admired this
'calculated bounce'. She told him: 'Kenneth, never underestimate the

effectiveness of simply just announcing something' (quoted in Baker, 1993, p. 192). A month later, at the North of England Education Conference, Baker fleshed out his proposal. He established its goal: to set a standard 'for all our schools, to provide teachers with detailed and precise objectives; to provide parents with clear information and to ensure continuity'. In Baker's view, after the demise of the 11-plus: 'some schools and LEAs were adrift in a sea of fashionable opinions about what children should not, rather than should be taught ... Whether children received good or poor education in the state sector had become a lottery. I knew our children deserved better ...' (Baker, 1993, p. 192).

The approach of a general election focused Conservative minds in the first half of 1987. The result was a continuation behind closed doors of the debate between Baker and the Prime Minister about the nature of the curriculum. In his autobiography Baker explains his commitment to a broad national curriculum in terms which neatly linked the cultural-restorationist perspective with that of the industrial-modernizers.

> At our meeting on 3 March the Prime Minister warned against over-elaboration of the Curriculum and said that she wanted to concentrate on the core subjects of English, maths and science. In the debates that took place between us both before and after the Election this proved to be the central issue. I believed that if we were to concentrate just upon the core subjects then schools would teach only to them and give much less prominence to the broader range which I felt was necessary. Some of the other subjects would be relegated or even ignored. I wanted to ensure that every boy and girl took not just science but also technology up to the age of sixteen. Furthermore, our national record in foreign languages was abysmal, since many children started to study them at eleven years old but gave them up at fourteen. I wanted to ensure that not only was the teaching of languages more relevant and more practical but that all children had to continue with them up to the age of sixteen.
>
> I also wanted to ensure that as regards history our children would leave school with real knowledge of what has happened in our country over the last 1,000 years. In many school visits I found children being taught about dinosaurs for the second or third time. It would have been a rather more helpful preparation for life if they could have distin-guished between Charles I and Cromwell, and known something about the Victorian Age and the Second World War, rather than being able to identify the differences between a brontosaurus and a tyrannosaurus. Geography too was important, but it was in danger of disappearing into the less rigorous form of environmental studies, rather than retaining its value as a more structured body of geographical knowledge starting with where Birmingham was in relation to London or Edinburgh. I also wanted to include art, music and sport in the National Curriculum. (Baker, 1993, p. 193)

In the event, the disagreement between the minister and his boss over the curriculum was suppressed for the duration of the election campaign at least. Meanwhile, Baker pressed ahead by setting up working groups on maths and science prior to the election, so that after a Conservative victory and the necessary legislation implementation could begin.

Shortly after the election a consultation document was published on the proposed ten-subject National Curriculum. As with other consultations to come, it emerged at the start of the summer holidays and required replies in the early days of the autumn term. This did nothing to endear Baker to the profession and its leaders, but that was, as far as he was concerned, unimportant. The document is misleadingly entitled 'The National Curriculum 5–16: A Consultation Document'. Baker had no intention of seriously consulting, as his own account of events reveals. The Bill was already being hastily drafted. Nevertheless, as a statement of government policy the consultation document is a key text. It argued that a national curriculum would help to raise standards by:

(i)   ensuring that all pupils study a broad and balanced range of subjects … and do not drop too early studies which may stand them in good stead later …

(ii) setting clear objectives for what children over the full range of ability should be able to achieve …

(iii) ensuring that all pupils regardless of sex, ethnic origin and geographical location have access to broadly the same good and relevant curriculum …

(iv) checking on progress towards those objectives and performance achieved at various stages … (DES/Welsh Office, 1987, pp. 3–4)

Apart from raising standards in this way, the document argued that children who moved from one area to another would gain in continuity. Though this is an obvious benefit, it is also a nice echo of Norman Tebbit's famous remark that the unemployed should get on their bikes. Finally, the document pointed out that a national curriculum would enable schools to be 'more accountable for the education they offer to their pupils individually and collectively'. Given the decade of debate which had preceded this document about accountability, that little phrase 'to their pupils' is interesting and ambiguous. Is the accountability 'to their pupils' or not? It depends how the sentence is read.

The document then sets out the now familiar components of the National Curriculum. First, there are the foundation subjects, which include the core subjects of English, mathematics and science. Baker's ongoing argument with Mrs Thatcher over breadth is fudged. Though Baker won in the end, in this document it says that 'the degree of definition in the requirements for each of these [ten] subjects will vary considerably, and will be greatest for the three core subjects'. The confusion over curriculum time, which became a feature of the debate later, is already apparent. We are told that:

> The Secretaries of State [for England and for Wales] do not intend to prescribe in legislation how much time should be allocated to each subject. But the foundation subjects commonly take up 80–90 per cent of the curriculum in schools where there is good practice. The Secretaries of State will take that as their starting point ...
>
> There will be time available beyond that required for the foundation subjects for religious education, and also for other popular subjects such as home economics ...

These glib assertions proved to be an inadequate basis for the curriculum to come.

The second element of the National Curriculum, the document pointed out, would be attainment targets: 'These will establish what children should normally be expected to know, understand and be able to do at around the ages of 7, 11, 14 and 16 and will enable the progress of each child to be measured against established national standards.' Attainment targets are mainly intended for the core subjects, it says in another gesture to the Prime Minister, but 'there will also be attainment targets for other foundation subjects where appropriate'. The chaos that later surrounded the articulation of GCSE with the National Curriculum is also foreshadowed here: 'Attainment targets for age 16 can be expected to take account of the GCSE criteria. But not all GCSE criteria are sufficiently specific and not all pupils will study all foundation subjects for public examination, so there will be other attainment targets ...' (p. 10). It could never have worked. The criticism of the GCSE criteria, a year before any pupil had sat a GCSE examination, is breathtaking, but at the time this was a side issue which went virtually unnoticed.

The third element of the proposed curriculum was to be the programmes of study, based, like the attainment targets, on proposals from subject working groups: 'They will reflect the attainment targets, and set out the overall content, knowledge, skills and processes relevant to today's needs which pupils should be taught in order to achieve them. They should also specify a minimum of content ...' (p. 10). This paragraph indicates a degree of ambiguity about the distinction between attainment targets and programmes of study. No wonder that each of the subsequent subject working groups found radically different ways of distinguishing between them.

The fourth element was to be assessment and examinations: 'The main purpose of such assessment will be to show what a pupil has learnt and mastered and to enable teachers and parents to ensure that he or she is making progress' (p. 11). Interestingly, the accountability purpose which came powerfully to the fore in later years is absent from this paragraph.

The proposals for the type of testing is also interesting. It is envisaged that: 'much of the assessment ... will be done by teachers as an integral part of normal classroom work. But at the heart of the assessment process there will be nationally prescribed tests done by all pupils to supplement the individual teachers' assessments. Teachers will administer and mark these but their marking ... will be externally moderated' (p. 11). The Task Group on Assessment and Testing (TGAT) had yet to be appointed, but its brief is set out here. When later ministers blamed TGAT for over-complicating the issue and not providing simple tests they conveniently forgot this paragraph from their own consultation document.

While differences between what was then proposed and what eventually emerged can be detected, the most startling fact about the consultation document is the extent to which what it set out eventually came to pass. The confusion over testing, which emerged later, could, for example, clearly have been predicted from this moment on. Most of all, the extent of prescription, which perhaps more than anything undermined the Baker curriculum, is plainly visible here at the starting line. No other country has ever attempted to prescribe attainment targets, programmes of study and national testing arrangements. One (or at the most two) of these three is normally considered sufficient to guarantee compliance. In some countries a non-statutory guide alone has proved effective. In this prescription it is evident that Kenneth Baker got his way. He had predicted that: 'If we did not have a full prescribed curriculum we would achieve very little improvement ... Those schools that were not up to scratch would simply carry on at they had been for a large part of the day' (Baker, 1993, p. 196). The proposals in the consultation reflected his determination to avoid this outcome. This fear coincided with the determination of DES officials to strengthen their grip on the education. Extensive prescription provided them with unprecedented influence. This was not a belt-and-braces approach to the curriculum, but two belts and two pairs of braces.

The consultation period was marked by the barefaced tokenism of the public consultation exercise and a fierce row behind the scenes between Baker and the Prime Minister. This was suspected at the time, but only the publication of Baker's memoirs reveals the full extent of it:

I believed that the prescribed curriculum should take up to 80 or 85 per cent of the teaching time ... but Margaret wanted the time for the National Curriculum to be reduced to 70 per cent. This issue came to a head in [a cabinet committee] on 28 October [1987] when the minutes recorded that art and music should not be compulsory and that the main curriculum should only take up 70 per cent of the time. Furthermore, attainment targets for all subjects other than the core should be dropped. I took the most unusual step of challenging these minutes in a personal minute to the Prime Minister ... I was challenging the accuracy of what was recorded as having been agreed. I was implying that the minutes reflected Margaret's personal views rather than the sense of the meeting ...

I was asked by the Prime Minister to withdraw my minute, but I refused to do so and saw her privately ... This was a tough meeting but I was simply not prepared to give in to a last minute rearguard action, even when waged by the Prime Minister herself. The broad-based curriculum was saved – for the time being. (Baker, 1993, p. 197)

It is obvious that we, the readers, are meant to conclude from this passage that Baker was a hero determined to stand up for what he believed, even against the Iron Lady at the height of her powers. Apart from the insight the passage provides into what was really happening behind the scenes, what is most interesting is the elision in Baker's argument. He takes it as axiomatic that a broadly based curriculum requires national prescription, i.e. that if art and music had not been compulsory, they would have been dropped. Many teachers reached the same conclusion and thus many subject specialists lobbied to have as much of their subject prescribed as possible. For the teachers' unions this created a sometimes unbearable tension in their responses. Teachers opposed excessive prescription, but also tended to oppose reduced prescription in any given subject area. Painful though it may be, it is hard to avoid the conclusion that National Curriculum implementation would have been less problematic and more effective if Margaret Thatcher had had her way.

While the Education Reform Bill wound its way through Parliament, Kenneth Baker began to implement the National Curriculum. He was a man in a hurry, and had no intention of waiting for the Bill to reach the statute book before he began the implementation phase. He recognized that this would be more difficult than establishing the principle of a national curriculum:

In former days, the Department would have set up a Working Group to proceed at the leisurely tempo of a Royal Commission ... But the decline of educational standards in Britain demanded swift action ... This was never going to be easy but I was determined to drive it through and I wanted the curriculum for each subject to be published for consultation within a year. I wanted to introduce the Maths and Science curriculum for five to eleven-year olds in September 1989. (Baker, 1993, pp.197–8)

In order to set the wheels in motion, Baker had set up Maths and Science Working Groups even before the 1987 election. Soon after it he asked Professor Paul Black of King's College, London, to chair the TGAT which was to establish a national model of assessment and testing.

In 1988, as the Act hit the statute book, Baker established the two advisory bodies which were to oversee the implementation of the

National Curriculum and assessment: the National Curriculum Council (NCC) and the School Examination and Assessment Council (SEAC). Their task, according to Baker, was to 'work very hard' to meet his tight timetable and 'to take along with [them] all the vested-interest groups including teachers ...' (Baker, 1993, p. 198). These replaced the School Curriculum and Development Committee (SCDC) and the Secondary Examinations Council (SEC) which had themselves replaced the Schools' Council only a few years earlier. Baker appointed Duncan Graham, former Chief Education Officer of Suffolk and Chief Executive of Humberside to be both Chair and Chief Executive of the NCC. He had proved his skills as someone who got things done, as Chair both of the National Steering Group (NSG) on schoolteacher appraisal and later of the mathematics working group, which was bogged down in conflict before Graham arrived and knocked various heads together. Baker liked his 'down-to-earth Scottish approach. He was not in thrall to the prejudices of academics and the fact that we have a National Curriculum at all owes much to his dogged determination' (Baker, p. 198). In this, at least, Baker's judgement is accurate. Philip Halsey, a retiring Deputy Secretary from the DES, was appointed to the parallel position at SEAC. He was a dry but highly skilled and efficient operator who lacked the flamboyance of Graham, frustrated people while he was in post and was then sorely missed by everyone after his abrupt departure in 1991.

In the 1989 publication 'From Policy to Practice' the government set down in some detail how it envisaged the National Curriculum and its assessment arrangements would be implemented:

> NCC has been asked to advise specifically on the whole curriculum context within which work on individual foundation subjects should be taken forward ... NCC will have a main responsibility for ensuring that elements of the National Curriculum fit together ... and make a coherent whole.

In retrospect, I am fascinated by that little word 'a'. The DES, it seems, was unwilling to suggest that the NCC should have *the* main responsibility for anything. The civil servants had not wanted the Act to include provision for the two councils, and throughout the implementation of the National Curriculum it fought against them for bureaucratic supremacy. SEAC's job, according to 'From Policy to Practice', was to advise on the assessment arrangements and to commission and oversee the development of standard assessment tasks. Both NCC and SEAC would advise on information outcomes and provide advice to LEAs on the training and dissemination implications of the National Curriculum. The process established for the arriving at the curricular content of each foundation subject was also described in 'From Policy to Practice':

The Secretary of State has established non-statutory working groups to do the initial work in recommending attainment targets and programmes of study for the foundation subjects. Their memberships include experts from a wide variety of educational backgrounds, and in the course of their work – each group has about a year to do its task – they are drawing on evidence and expertise from throughout the education service. The Mathematics and Science Working Groups have already made recommendations for all key stages covering primary education. The English Working Group and the Design and Technology Group are continuing their work. The History Group has recently been set up, the Geography Group will be established at Easter 1989 and the Modern Foreign Languages Group in July 1989. Work on music, art and physical education is likely to start in the summer of 1990. Each group has a timetable that allows for sensibly phased implementation.

The working groups' recommendations form the basis for the formal proposals which the Secretary of State must make about attainment targets and programmes of study for each subject. NCC is required to undertake statutory consultations about those proposals, reporting the results of consultations to the Secretary of State and making recommendations to him about what should go in statutory Orders. NCC may consult as widely as it wishes but *must* consult representatives of teachers, local authorities and school governors. NCC has to publish its subsequent recommendations, alongside a summary of the views expressed during consultation. The Secretary of State must then convert NCC's recommendations into draft Orders, and publish his reasons if he proposes to make Orders which are significantly different. Those previously consulted by NCC must be consulted about the draft Orders. Following that – subject to Parliament's approval – the Orders will be turned into binding legal requirements. This full and open process of consultation means that a great many people and organisations have the opportunity to contribute to the shape of the final Orders, as the consultation exercise on the first proposals for mathematics and science has demonstrated. (DES, 1989b)

The interesting aspect of this process is that it provides the appearance of consultation, while in reality ensuring that both the DES and ministers kept a firm hold on the process. Ministers, after all, appointed the members of the working groups and of the NCC, while the DES provided the secretariat for each of the working groups and had representatives present at both working groups and NCC meetings. HMI, which had differed from the DES in emphasis over the curriculum throughout the 1980s, is afforded a position of much less influence than officials. In the section on 'Who Does What' in 'From Policy to Practice' the only role allotted to HMI is that of monitoring and evaluation. In fact, it too had representatives at the working group and council meetings and made significant contributions. Nevertheless, the tensions between HMI, the DES and the Councils added to the tensions in the implementation process: those same tensions also ensured that from time to time those outside this charmed circle received glimpses – like breaks in the cloud – of the real political conflicts, as they spilled out into the open.

On 1 September 1989, the first pupils began following National Curriculum provisions in maths, science and English in Key Stage 1 (ages 5–7) and maths and science in Key Stage 2 (ages 7–11). 'From Policy to Practice' described how it was intended that, from that historic day, the National Curriculum would be implemented progressively until the mid-1990s. The final act of implementation, according to the appendices, would be that of Key Stages 2 and 4 Standard Assessment Tests (SATs) in music, art and PE in the mid-1990s. Like many other proposals in 'From Policy to Practice', that of course never came to pass.

The professional response

The main reaction among teachers' union leaders – both elected executive members and headquarters staff – to all of this was, if my memory serves me correctly, one of disbelief. The idea that there could be such levels of prescription; the idea that change could happen so fast; the idea that the Schools' Council philosophy had gone for ever; the idea that teachers' leaders would be marginalized; the idea that something as important as a national curriculum could be put out for consultation in July with responses in September: all of this seemed almost literally incredible.

Yet, in spite of this enormity, the National Curriculum was not, in 1989, the top priority for the teacher organizations. Certainly it was important, but the implementation of teachers' nationally imposed contracts – still only two years old – remained an anxiety, as of course did the question of pay. More important perhaps than any of these was the perceived threat posed by Local Management of Schools (LMS) to traditional bargaining structures. Once LMS was implemented, the defence of members through deals with LEAs and hard won agreements at LEA level, and the possibility of redeployment when jobs needed saving, were all at stake. The waxing power of school governing bodies and the waning influence of LEAs undermined all the traditional levers of influence. As if that was not enough, a national scheme of teacher appraisal was proposed in that summer of 1989. Though it had the backing of union leaders, it was too highly controversial. It would be fair to say that the union leaderships were not sure which way to turn, but certainly at this stage the National Curriculum had not yet become the chief concern of their general secretaries. They remained focused on matters which had traditionally been top of their priorities, and those of their members: tenure, pay and conditions of service.

Almost as soon as they had been established, the NCC and SEAC had established low-key termly consultative meetings between themselves and representatives of the six teachers' unions. Duncan Graham, who as Chair of the NSG on schoolteacher appraisal was well known to union education officers, and Alan Evans, the NUT's Education Officer until 1989 (and Vice-Chair of the NSG), had been instrumental in setting up these consultative forums. They became increasingly important, particularly at the NCC, for two reasons. Firstly, they established a set of working relationships between the Councils' staff and teacher union representatives. Thus, informal channels of communication between unions and the decision-makers began to flow again, albeit at a relatively low level at first. Union leaders, even when they are unable to change the course of events, like at least to be well informed. Similarly, NCC staff found the meetings a valuable sounding board not only for shaping decisions, but for gathering ammunition for their increasingly fierce guerrilla war with DES officials.

Secondly, and perhaps most importantly in the long run, the meetings enabled representatives of teachers' unions, below the level of general secretary, to forge close and trusting working relationships among themselves which, in the crucial summer of 1993, enabled them to promote a common agenda for the revision of the curriculum with Sir Ron Dearing. The alliance was greatly strengthened by the presence at these meetings of representatives from the various national organizations of independent schools (see Sheila Dainton's chapter below). The rule was that the six unions could each put up two representatives, while these others could put up one. At first, some union representatives took umbrage at sharing meetings with these often tiny organizations, but in the end they wisely decided that it would be advantageous for them to remain in the same meeting rather than meet NCC officials separately. In practice, it rarely proved difficult to achieve unanimous agreement. Occasionally – as over GCSE science – there were differences, but these were minor compared to the agreement on the major issues such as the process for making curriculum decisions, the extent of prescription, and a rejection of the narrow ideological concerns which increasingly dictated government policy. The key to the effectiveness of the teachers' side in these meetings was a decision taken in late 1989 to change the structure of the day so that there would be time for the teachers' representatives to meet together in advance. So, for instance, they might meet alone for an hour and a half before lunch, and then meet the NCC or SEAC staff for two hours after lunch. The result was that there was time to hammer out common positions, share out responsibilities among the different organizations and build up trust. At the NUT – of which the author was a representative – representatives used to plan their approach to the meetings beforehand, usually on the train to York for NCC meetings. One or two priorities would be chosen, the support of colleagues would be sought in the teachers' pre-meeting and their views would then be presented, on behalf of all the organizations, in the afternoon. I guess the other organizations took a similar approach.

Meanwhile, inside each of the teachers' unions, to varying degrees, there was a growing understanding that, in an utterly changed policy world, new approaches to policy formation and advocacy were necessary. There were a number of consequences of this re-evaluation of both strategy and tactics which have had a profound effect on the ability of the unions to exercise effective influence. Union leaders began to recognize that changing policy in relation to the curriculum would take time and required them not only to provide a critique, but to suggest alternatives and ultimately a set of practical solutions.

In the development of union approaches, there are close parallels with Hewton's (1986) analysis of local government responses to crisis. The first stage in the crisis in the case of unions was to criticize and reject. Hence, when the Schools' Council was abolished in 1984, the NUT at first refused to have anything to do with its successors, the SCDC and the SEC. Once it became clear that a revival of the Schools' Council was not likely, this position became untenable and the NUT opened up informal channels of communication. Hewton characterizes this kind of response as 'defensive'. The second stage of response was to recognize that the government's reform proposals would not easily be reversed and thus, instead of straight opposition, the unions began a phase of pragmatic accommodation. They chipped away at the government's policy proposals and only gave way when they had no choice. Hewton characterizes this stage as 'pragmatic'. This was a demoralizing process and often resulted in the unions being perceived to be reactive, negative and weak. It also convinced the government that all it had to do was drive forward its policies and eventually, however reluctantly, the unions would fall into line. Some in government even drew the ultimately fatal conclusion from this process that the unions no longer mattered. To misquote Kaiser Wilhelm, they took the view that 'There are no more unions: only teachers.'

The third phase of the development of union response was what might be called 'reformist' or 'strategic' (Hewton, 1986; Barber, 1992). Crucially, this involved rejecting the underlying assumption of both the previous positions, i.e. that the implicit goal of policy was to return the situation to the state of affairs before the government embarked on its reforms. This deeply conservative goal had become increasingly unrealistic. In relation to the curriculum, for example, it meant defending teacher control over the curriculum even when, in extreme cases as at William Tyndale, it had proved to be indefensible. It also meant defending a *status quo*, in which large numbers of young people consistently failed, and left school with nothing to show for it but a bruised ego and an antipathy to learning.

Once the unions began to look forward, their prospects brightened. They began, in relation to the National Curriculum at any rate, to ask a new question: What sort of curriculum does the country need in the twenty-first century and how do we move towards it? This opened up a more fruitful critique of government policy and one which parents and governors were much more likely to support. In the case of the NUT, the publication in 1990 of 'A Strategy for the Curriculum' was symbolic of this shift in attitude. After that there was no more hankering after the old comfortable days of partnership; instead there was a steady and trenchant criticism of government for proposing a curriculum which could not work. Linked to the critique were constructive proposals for change. Other teachers' organizations were undertaking a similar process in their different ways. Thus, when the NCC officials talked about 'the basics' that ministers were fleetingly so fond of, union representatives argued for the basics of the twenty-first century, not those of the 1950s.

Given this new approach to policy development, it became necessary to provide evidence for the case against the government. Prior to the 1988 Act, there had normally been formal evaluations – often jointly overseen by government and teachers – of major initiatives, as in the case, for example, of the teacher-appraisal pilot schemes. This ceased to be the case with the National Curriculum. When the government did commission evaluations, these tended to be published long after the event, or in some cases not at all. The unions therefore began to commission research projects or evaluations themselves. Of course, they monitored developments through the membership in any case, but this evidence tended to be dismissed as partial. Research commissioned from academic or consultancy organizations proved much more effective. Much of the best work on the early National Curriculum resulted from this development. Perhaps the most outstanding studies that emerged from this process were those on primary schools commissioned from Warwick University by the Association of Teachers and Lecturers (ATL) (see Sheila Dainton's chapter below) and the study commissioned from Coopers and Lybrand by the NUT entitled 'The Costs of the National Curriculum'. Both made a major impact and both contributed to the growing public relations conflict between government and the profession.

Increasingly, the unions recognized, too, the need for effective public relations and, above all, for having allies among parents and governors. From 1990 onwards the unions focused on building up such alliances. In 1991, for example, the NUT, along with the National Association of Head Teachers (NAHT), won the support of four parent and governor organizations for their proposals on the assessment of 7-year olds, and two deputations to ministers involved all of these organizations. The following year the NUT pointed out to its school representatives that where teachers, parents and governors in a particular school were united 'it was virtually invincible'. The 1993 test boycott proved that this was true.

If this was the increasingly effective response of teachers' union leaders, what was the state of affairs among teachers themselves? The answer almost certainly is that, during the early phases of National Curriculum implementation, teachers, especially in primary schools, felt over-burdened, overworked, undervalued and confused. The advice to them from union documents, however well thought out, provided little respite. Whether or not individual teachers felt supported through the process depended very much on the qualities of their headteacher and the LEA. Though the NCC and SEAC provided many excellent publications, these often became part of the problem: there were simply too many instructions hitting schools in too short a space of time. And there was no doubt that, increasingly, teachers were overworked. A series of studies commissioned by unions suggested teachers were working around fifty hours per week and headteachers considerably more. The most pressured teachers of all were those who taught 7-year olds, especially during the first full run of SATs in 1991. Moreover, as teachers pointed out to an NUT survey on those tests, it was much more than a workload issue: 'For three weeks all break times have been spent on ... SATs ...'; 'Recording and preparation for the next day took a minimum of 2 hours per night'; 'I can only hope that no Year 2 teacher ever again has to suffer the indignity of having their professionalism questioned' (NUT, 1992). The third quotation hits the nail on the head. What teachers found so demoralizing was the direct attack on their professionalism that the new curriculum and its associated tests represented. Though ministers sometimes paid lip service to teachers, the extent of prescription and the absence of consultation combined to form a calculated attack on the idea of a profession. This was painful to many teachers.

The government completely failed to win hearts and minds. On the contrary, it alienated them. Workload is not just a matter of hours and days: it is a question of motivation. For a cause to which they were commit-ted, fifty hours a week might have been acceptable; for a cause which was perceived as an attack on the profession, the workload was an intolerable burden. The government at that time never appeared to understand this message, though it is at the heart of virtually every management manual written in the last fifteen years. Ironically, what saved the National Curri-culum was that very professionalism which the government threatened to undermine. The combination of teachers' sense of duty, their commit-ment to pupils and the often effective support of LEAs ensured that, for all its flaws, the National Curriculum was implemented. Its faults were most apparent in Key Stage 2, but even there, once it was in place, teachers began to see the benefits of the National Curriculum. There was value in the development of a language – shared across the country – in which the curriculum could be discussed. There was value, too, in gaining insights into national expectations. The over-prescription, the constant meddling by ministers, the over-hasty and under-funded implementa-tion time-table and the absence of consultation were all serious problems, but the overall concept of a national curriculum steadily gained ground.

A survey of teacher opinion in the *Times Educational Supplement* (TES) on 27 March 1992 showed that teachers believed that the National Curriculum, of all the government's reforms, had done the most to raise standards.

By then, enough teachers had sufficient familiarity with the National Curriculum to have a clear view of its problems. This presented them with a dilemma: they wanted the problems solving; yet finding and implementing solutions would add to what appeared to be the most serious problem of all: the pace and extent of change. Unions therefore found themselves under conflicting pressure. Should they stick with what they had in order to reduce the pressure of change? Or should they seek a comprehensive revision, in spite of what that entailed in terms of further change and uncertainty? Key Stage 3 teachers, and perhaps Key Stage 1 teachers, might have settled for the former. Key Stage 4 teachers had problems of their own which were only in part caused by the National Curriculum. The real pressure for curriculum change came from Key Stage 2 teachers who rightly believed that they could never successfully implement so prescriptive and detailed a curriculum across ten subjects within the confines of the traditional junior classroom. For this reason, the NCC itself embarked on a revision of Key Stage 2 in the autumn of 1992. This resulted in the publication in January 1993 of the NCC's advice to the Secretary of State on 'The National Curriculum at Key Stages 1 and 2' (NCC, 1993). It concluded that:

> ... teachers broadly support the principle of a National Curriculum but consider that it is proving too complex and over-prescriptive. They are particularly concerned that the collective weight of content ... at Key Stage 2 is leading to curriculum overload and superficial teaching ... We conclude that changes to the content of the primary curriculum will be needed in due course as part of a considered programme of curriculum evolution. (NCC, 1993, p. 1)

Recognition of the difficulties was given no sense of urgency, even at this stage. In spite of the pressure from teachers and their organizations, the document still argued: 'It is not a programme [of reform] that can or should be rushed ... We will hold a further series of seminars to promote thinking' (NCC, 1993, p. 3). Given the rapid pace of change when politicians themselves wanted something done, this lack of 'rush' can be taken to indicate that little political priority was attached at this stage to making sense of Key Stage 2. The timetable for revision envisaged by the NCC clearly involved years rather than months. The measured, almost complacent, tones of that NCC document represent the last moment when the government and its allied agencies can have really believed that they were in control of events. In fact, they were heading for a fall.

The seeds of destruction

The seeds of the crisis of 1993 are to be found in part in the nature of the curriculum that had emerged by then and in part in the controversial and often ill-considered testing programme. Most of all, in my view, they are to be found in the fundamentally flawed process of decision-making which surrounded the National Curriculum and its assessment arrangements. By 1992–3 this caused an unprecedented and extraordinary combination of arrogance and error. The gap between the decision-makers' views of what was happening (and what was possible) and the reality in the schools had become a chasm.

The process for making the curriculum was flawed, as we have seen, from the outset. Priority had never been given to involving or even effectively consulting teachers. The timetable for implementation laid down by Kenneth Baker was always pressured and the extent of political and DES control was excessive. Consultation with teachers would not and should not have implied doing what teachers wanted (assuming they could agree). It is right that, for a democratically elected government, some things will be non-negotiable. On the other hand, without effective consultation, successful implementation is impossible. As the process was unfolding, the extent and nature of problems could only be guessed at, but the evidence of their existence – in poor or altered decisions – was extensive. There were at least four separate flaws in the decision-making process. Though in the day-to-day reality they were all of a piece, they can be separated out for analytical purposes.

The first was excessive, direct political interference. There were a number of notable examples. Duncan Graham, in conversation with the author, claimed – perhaps apocryphally – that when Mrs Thatcher returned his copy of the draft English order having read it over breakfast, it still had her marmalade on its corners. It ought to be true because it symbolizes the extent to which ministers, and sometimes even the Prime Minister, took an interest in the details of the National Curriculum. In doing so, they not only put personal prejudice before effective implementation, they also set a precedent for all future ministers of whatever party. Between the world wars, a Conservative government had shied away from creating a national curriculum because it feared what a Labour government might do if it took hold of such a profound and important lever on the future. Presumably, Baker and his successors in the early 1990s believed that Labour would never win again. Thus, Baker personally insisted on a powerful dose of English history and plenty of poetry. He argued in his autobiography: 'I also wanted to ensure that as regards history our children would leave school with real knowledge of what has happened in our country over the last 1000 years.' While that view is unexceptionable, when the proposals emerged Kenneth Baker took an extra close interest because:

History had been the subject of my degree, and I had produced an anthology of poetry which told the history of England from Boadicea to Elizabeth II … The early drafts of the history curriculum arrived before I moved [to become Chairman of the Conservative Party] and I was disappointed with the lack of emphasis on the teaching of hard facts. Both of my successors were to make changes to the history curriculum. Ken Clarke decided that the history curriculum had to end twenty years before the present day … While there had certainly been too much emphasis upon current affairs in history teaching, this step seemed to rigid a demarcation. (Baker, 1993, p. 206)

It is interesting to note that Baker did not agree with Clarke's decision, but more revealing is the fact that crucial decisions about the nature of a national curriculum were – because of the high degree of centralization – left to the personal prejudices of each passing minister. Since the Dearing Report, ministers have been much wiser and more circumspect, but the powers remain in their hands.

Divisions among the key players were the second flaw in the process. Institutional conflicts between the DES and the NCC, SEAC and OFSTED have already been identified. So, too, has the division between Thatcher and Baker over the degree of curriculum prescription. There were other tensions. The NCC, for instance worried about SEAC in effect deciding the curriculum through its testing decisions; the assessment tail sometimes appeared to wag the curriculum dog. Meanwhile, NCC and HMI disagreed about how to evaluate the implementation of the curriculum. HMI believed evaluation was its job. The NCC, on the other hand, wanted to commission independent research. In this disagreement HMI tended to have the support of the DES and ministers, since independent research had a nasty habit of costing money and arriving at unwelcome conclusions. As Duncan Graham commented after his resignation: 'Another casualty has been that of proper independent research, evaluation and monitoring. The NCC was not permitted to undertake the broad, disinterested research which I envisaged when appointed' (Barber and Graham, 1992, p. 9).

The most constant division was that between the two advisory councils and the DES. DES civil servants carefully shadowed every action of NCC and SEAC; they attended meetings, commented on draft documents and used a range of bureaucratic devices to ensure that they – though they would say 'ministers' – got their way. This was a game at which they excelled. One tactic was to begin an intervention in a meeting with words such as 'Ministers would be reluctant to see …' or 'Ministers could not countenance …'. This could often be translated as the civil servant guessing that ministers might be opposed to a given proposal, but others at the meeting had no way of checking whether or not ministers had really expressed that opinion. Another parallel device was to prevent others from having direct access to ministers. The dispute between the DES and NCC over cross-curricular themes provided the classic example of this bureaucratic manoeuvring. In his fascinating record of those times, Duncan Graham gives his own account of a sequence of events which can only be described as bizarre. First he establishes the background:

> During the first six months of NCC I found myself being kept away from Ministers although I had been led to believe by Kenneth Baker – and I am sure he meant it – that I would see him quite frequently. It soon became clear that ... I was only going to be brought before him on stage-managed occasions.
> ... While described by some people outside the Council as the man in charge of the curriculum I was in reality a prisoner of the system ... (Graham, 1993, p. 19)

He then turns to describe the crisis. The NCC had embarked on the production of five documents of advice on cross-curricular themes. It had an explicit brief to examine the whole curriculum so, this might have been thought to be non-controversial. In fact, officials and ministers increasingly took the view that the focus should be on the ten National Curriculum subjects and that everything else was a distraction:

> Then the roof fell in. A posse of civil servants descended on York to tell NCC that it could not continue work on nor publish the five booklets ... Clearly alarmed by what he had been told by the civil servants, Kenneth Baker wrote a detailed two page letter to the Council in May 1989 in which he told it to abandon [this work] ... In the future nothing should go to formal meetings until it had been seen and approved by the Secretary of State. Here was the question of independence in a nutshell ... At that point I decided that I had to see Baker alone and telephoned him at home ... He showed great concern and said that we should meet urgently without civil servants. (Graham, 1993, pp. 19–21)

Since both happened to be due in Wales soon after, they agreed to meet at a hotel there:

> A helicopter was waiting for Baker in a field behind the hotel. I went with some trepidation as I wondered whom he would have with him. Dressed in his running gear, he came out of the hotel to meet me and shook me warmly by the hand. We went into the hotel and found a room where we talked over coffee. We started with the letter and its implications. He looked at it and could not believe he had signed it. It was one of those magic moments in life ... Still talking, we walked out to the helicopter. He said he was very shaken and angry by what had happened and that we should meet more regularly. (Graham, 1993, p. 21)

The five documents duly appeared, but the story reveals starkly the influence of civil servants and the lengths to which even people in apparently powerful positions like Graham had to go to in order to make things happen. In the end, even as tough a character as Graham depended on his personal rapport with Baker. Once Baker had gone, the civil servants were able once again to assume the ascendancy.

This leads directly to the third flaw in the decision-making process. There were regular changes of personnel in key positions at ministerial level, among DES officials and at both the NCC and the SEAC (see Sheila Dainton's chapter below). Few people in positions of influence survived long enough to have a clear overview or to establish consistent lines of policy. In its life of five years, for example, the NCC had three chairmen and two chief executives and none of its deputy chief executives was in post for much more than two years. A similar story could be told at SEAC. At Council level, members came and went as though they were stuck in a revolving door. Over the same six years (1988–94) there were four Secretaries of State for Education and three permanent secretaries at the DES. The department even changed its name and became the DFE during this period. In 1995 it was merged with the Department of Employment and changed its name again. Ironically, in the same five years the staffing of the teacher unions was very stable.

Thus, by the time Sir Ron Dearing arrived on the scene in March 1993, it was union people who had the historical perspective, not officials at either the DFE or in the two Councils. The instability, especially at ministerial level, was partly responsible for the swings in policy direction. Perhaps when Dearing arrived on the scene it became, for the first time, an advantage, since there was no one who had been around long enough to have a vested interest in defending the indefensible curriculum which this bewildering array of individuals had created.

All of this was greatly compounded throughout the process, culminating in 1991–2, by an extraordinary and completely unnecessary secrecy, which was the fourth flaw. Ministers, from Kenneth Clarke onwards, tended to pack the NCC and SEAC Councils with representatives of the Centre for Policy Studies (CPS) and the other right-wing pressure groups whose prejudices overshadowed any expertise they might have had. The cloak-and-dagger atmosphere reached a climax in the summer of 1991 when, within a week, Duncan Graham and Philip Halsey were sacked and replaced by, respectively, David Pascall and Brian (Lord) Griffiths. Both of these had been influential advisers at 10 Downing Street and both were linked with the right-wing pressure groups. Though David Pascall strove to establish a degree of legitimacy among teachers, Griffiths never did, with, ultimately, disastrous consequences. An atmosphere of intrigue coloured every debate from the moment of their appointment, until Sir Ron Dearing replaced them and ushered in a refreshing and long-overdue openness.

One example will suffice. During 1992 ministers – lobbied from the right-wing pressure groups – decided that the National Curriculum

English Order was not robust enough. There was, they argued, insufficient emphasis on phonics in the teaching of reading, a lack of clarity about standard English and a need for a prescribed list of texts which became known as the canon. This was a political decision taken about a curriculum order that, on the whole, was working well. Nevertheless, it was little surprise when the Pascall-chaired NCC published a consultation document broadly agreeing with the concerns expressed by ministers. In it, the NCC quoted from an evaluation of the English Order being undertaken for them by Bridie Raban at Warwick University. Though they quoted from it, they did not publish the full text of the Warwick evaluation. When representatives of the unions asked for this formality to be undertaken, their request was refused. Yet surely, in any kind of demo- cratic debate, a document quoted by one set of protagonists ought to be open to the inspection of the others. The view that the NCC might have quoted misleadingly was, after all, not entirely unreasonable in the circum- stances. In the end, in spite of repeated requests, the Warwick evaluation was not made public until it had ceased to be relevant. I did, however, manage to obtain a copy of it during the critical period, not from Warwick University which, in spite of intense pressure, remained honourably loyal to its contract, but from a member of staff at the NCC who gave me one in their underground car park during the autumn of 1992. For a moment 'Deep Throat' lived again! The document said little that was unexpected, but the affair reveals how far the decision-making process had shifted from anything that might be described as rational.

Given the nature of some of the NCC members and the pressure put on them by DFE officials, it was hardly surprising that such good, professional staff lived in a climate of anxiety; it was a climate which made it extremely difficult for them to build trusting relations with exter- nal organizations. To their credit, some of them managed to do so in spite of the pressure.

Chris Woodhead, in his chapter below, gives a different and cogent explanation of why the English Order was revised: the problem was that in the atmosphere of secrecy no such rational case was ever likely to be taken at face value.

By 1993, as a result of these four flaws, but also because of the peculiar incompetence of John Patten, appointed Secretary of State for Education after the Conservative election victory in April 1992, the curriculum and assessment policy was about to spiral out of control.

The crisis for the curriculum

John Patten inherited from his predecessor, Kenneth Clarke, an unenvi- able legacy. Leaving aside wider issues of policy such as the governance of grant-maintained schools and the need for still more legislation, the

National Curriculum was already riddled with problems. There was huge resentment among practitioners. Worse still for Patten, the associated testing programme was about to extend into the secondary sector. A consummate politician would have been stretched by the task ahead. John Patten, in fact, proved anything but consummate. He had a brief honeymoon in which people remembered that, as a Fellow of Hertford College, Oxford, he was himself an educator and that his primary age daughter attended a state school in Westminster. But from the moment he turned down an invitation to attend the NAHT conference a few weeks after he had been in post, his political judgement was increasingly open to question.

After providing some background on the implementation of the government's assessment and testing policy and on the developing controversy over English teaching, this section attempts to explain the unfolding events between the summers of 1992 and 1993. These were, without doubt, the most disastrous months of policy-making in the postwar era.

The report, which underpinned the government's original approach to testing, became known in the education world simply as 'TGAT' – the Task Group on Assessment and Testing. Paul Black, Professor of Science Education at King's College, London, and later the first Vice-Chair of the NCC, was asked to chair TGAT, which was established in July 1987, before the Education Reform Bill had even been drafted. Its task was to advise on the practical considerations governing assessment within the National Curriculum. TGAT recommended that children should be 'assessed using a mixture of standard assessment tasks, more narrowly focused tests and teacher assessments' (Gipps, 1988, p. 8). Each subject was to be built round ten levels covering the 5–16 age range: level two was to be the expected 7-year old performance and level four the expected 11-year old performance, and so on. The report proposed publication of each school's distribution of performance at age 11, 14 and 16, but not 7. The TGAT report emphazised the importance of educationally sound assessment and of teachers' moderation of results across schools similar to that which characterized GCSE assessment. Several of the contentious issues which later emerged were already apparent at this stage. How would the levels work in practice and how would comparability across subjects be ensured? Would the proposed moderation system receive the investment it required to make it work? And on the day of publication Kenneth Baker himself suggested that the proposals 'appear complicated and costly'. Perhaps most fundamentally of all, TGAT's view that one assessment system could be both formative and diagnostic on the one hand, and summative and evaluative on the other built a tension into the proposals which ultimately contributed to its destruction. Essentially, TGAT attempted to produce a system of assessment which would have credibility among sceptical professionals, while simultaneously meeting the government's political demand for accountability. In the end, this circle proved impossible to square.

In 1990 the first SATs for 7-year olds were piloted in about 2 per cent of primary schools. The tasks were designed to flow from the curriculum and thus took many hours to implement. Though the designers of the tasks saw educational merit in them, they failed to impress either the government which saw them as unnecessarily complicated and expensive, or teachers who groaned at both the workload and the loss of curriculum time. In short, the government did not like them because they wanted simpler tests: teachers did not like them because they did not want tests at all. The stage was set for the first phase of confrontation over the government's assessment programme in 1991, the first year in which all 7-year olds were tested. At the NUT's Easter conference, the militant wing of the union overturned a recommendation of the Executive and voted for a boycott. In the ensuing ballot, however, the overwhelming majority of the teachers involved followed the Executive's advice and voted against a boycott, while expressing their hostility to the SATs as a concept. The union was urged to continue its campaign against them.

All the unions monitored the effect of the tests carefully and some published research evaluating their impact (see Sheila Dainton's chapter below). The NUT published a polemical report based on its own evaluation exercise. Entitled 'Miss, the Rabbit Ate the Floating Apple' (NUT, 1992), it contained not only many stories from the battlefront, but also some powerful research findings which the government could not lightly dismiss. SEAC had said the SATs should take 30 hours of class time; according to the NUT survey they took an average of 52 hours. Three-quarters of teachers reported a detrimental effect on pupil behaviour and around 90 per cent of teachers claimed that they had learnt nothing new from the tasks. The official evaluation, carried out at Leeds University, was somewhat more positive, though it too suggested that the 30-hour time limit was inadequate. However, like many official evaluations of that era it was published too late to have any impact on the rapidly developing policy.

That same year – 1991 – Key Stage 3 tests were piloted and dismissed characteristically by Kenneth Clarke as 'complicated nonsense'. The combination of this view from the politicians and the understandable complaints from teachers about the length of time SATs were taking pointed almost inevitably to simpler tests. However, simpler tests are much less likely to be either valid or reliable, and the grounds for opposition to the tests – the word increasingly used instead of SATs from 1991 on – began to shift on to educational grounds. For 1992 two sets of tests were planned. All 7-year olds would be given refined, simpler tests; secondary schools were given the option of participating in the Key Stage 3 pilot tests for maths and science. In the event, 80 per cent chose to try them, presumably on the grounds that, since they were coming anyway, it would be beneficial to have experience of them. The testing period ran reasonably smoothly. Few teachers at either Key Stage 1 or Key Stage 3 liked the tests, but the number of complaints to union headquarters – a good guide to whether a policy is causing outrage – was relatively few. A betting person at the end of that summer would have put money on the tests at both Key Stage 1 and Key Stage 3 being fully established the following summer. Instead, the controversial politics of the teaching of English, combined with the crass incompetence of Lord Griffiths, the Chairman of SEAC, and of the Secretary of State John Patten, upturned the apple cart.

The English curriculum

The teaching of English had been controversial for years. There were ongoing debates about how to teach reading, about the extent to which spelling and grammar should be taught, about standard and non-standard English and about the extent to which literature should emphasize the nineteenth-century classics and, of course, Shakespeare. The equal opportunities thrust of the 1980s had emphasized the importance of valuing a variety of cultures and selecting books accordingly. There had been powerful arguments for the development of 'oracy' and valuing dialect or non-standard versions of the language, and for a generation the importance of encouraging young people to express their feelings and powers of imagination in writing had been emphasized. The government and the right-wing pressure groups that hovered in its vicinity were deeply suspicious of this liberal approach. Kenneth Baker expressed his anxiety clearly in his autobiography:

> I was particularly concerned about the teaching of English ... I suggested that we begin our review of the curriculum by establishing an inquiry into the nature of English with the objective of establishing what should be taught in our schools about our language. Such a question could not arise in France, where schoolchildren receive as a matter of course a uniform grounding in their language, its development, structure and grammar. (Baker, 1993, p. 190)

Objectively speaking, Baker had a point. There is an ambiguity about English attitudes to English which simply does not arise in France. He was also justifiably concerned about the levels of functional illiteracy among adults. He was wrong, however, in assuming that his gut instincts were necessarily the solution. Meanwhile, the English-teaching lobby was strongly attached to its own pedagogical position for which there was a powerful case as long as the teaching associated with it was of sufficient quality and rigour. It was weak when the ideology became a smokescreen for poor or shallow teaching. Baker's critique of their position was characteristically exaggerated out of all proportion. Teaching such as that in France, he argued, '… had virtually ceased in British schools, where teaching had fallen victim to the ludicrous political fashion which argued that language was an instrument of class … there was therefore to be no "correct" form of language. Anything was acceptable …' (Baker, 1993, pp. 190–1).

So it was that, early in 1987, the Committee of Inquiry under Sir John Kingman, Vice-Chancellor of Bristol University (and inevitably a scientist) was established. In March 1988 it reported, and to many in the field appeared to have cleverly bridged the gap between the politicians and the professionals. This was not Baker's view: '… the Kingman Report proved a disappointment because one of its conclusions was that standard English should be regarded as merely one of several dialects … It appeared that even guardians of standards had become infected with fashionable nonsense' (Baker, 1993, p. 191). In other words, the inquiry was a waste of time because it did not agree with Kenneth Baker, an odd view to hold, since there seems little point in having an inquiry if you already know the answers in advance. Baker and his successors learnt their lesson from this, and as a result the National Curriculum working groups had fewer professionals and less independence. Appointments to agencies were carefully vetted and, on the whole, independent research, evaluations or inquiries were shunned.

When it came to establishing the English National Curriculum, Baker appointed Brian Cox, Professor of English at Manchester and a former member of the Kingman Committee, to chair it. The profession feared the worst, for Cox was best known as one of the authors of the Black Papers which had spearheaded the attack on progressivism in the late 1960s and 1970s. Cox, however, surprised everyone by producing proposals which broadly speaking met the political objections to Kingman without upsetting the teaching profession. It was a masterly piece of consensus-building. On the question of the literary canon, Cox's first report in November 1988 listed the kind of books that might be expected to appear in a primary school library without suggesting that they should be prescribed. Inevitably, the debate over it focused on two missing stars. In the press Cox became, as he later put it, 'the villain who put his knife into Noddy and his boot into Biggles' (Cox, 1992, p. 248). Kenneth Baker told him later that 'the decision to exclude Enid Blyton had proved a brilliant ploy to attract attention away from our more serious controversial proposals' (Cox, 1992, p. 248). In the final report the list was simply excluded to avoid further controversy. Nevertheless the report insisted that pupils did learn about the cultural heritage. Some Shakespeare – but unspecified – was a requirement. Pupils were also required to study 'a wide range of literary forms', including short stories, poems, plays and novels. They were to encounter literary works written in English from across the world and to have contact with pre-twentieth-century English writing. On the highly charged question of standard English, Cox describes how his report eventually ended up at Number 10 Downing Street, for Margaret Thatcher to peruse: 'In the attainment targets for writing we had written "Use standard English, where appropriate." The Prime Minister asked for "where appropriate" to be deleted ... I re-wrote the sentence as follows: "Use standard English (except in contexts where non-standard forms are needed for literary purposes, e.g. in dialogue, in a story or playscript)"' (Cox, 1992, p. 258). This is an interesting example of how compromise can often be reached by being more specific rather than more vague.

Cox's primary school proposals were published first in November 1988 and his secondary school proposals followed some months later. The first report caused agitated comings and goings between his group, the DES and the NCC. Duncan Graham describes in his own account of events how Cox's proposals needed 'toughening up'. He made some changes which did not please Cox, and which at one stage were not apparently satisfactory to ministers. Just before the proposals were due to go to Graham's Council a civil servant rang him and told him that the meeting should be cancelled and the report re-written, but he called her bluff and the document went ahead (Graham, 1993, p. 50). The secondary school report caused less controversy, partly because it seems from Graham's account that he and Cox worked more closely together, and partly because, by the time it emerged, the calm and pragmatic John MacGregor was Secretary of State for Education. MacGregor's appointment in the autumn of 1989 ushered in a period of relative calm in the tortured and turbulent world of English teaching, but a year later he was on the move again, replaced by the no-nonsense specialist Kenneth Clarke. A few weeks later Margaret Thatcher was toppled and John Major became Prime Minister.

In his first speech on education in July 1991 (delivered inevitably to a Centre for Policy Studies Conference), Major found a new angle of attack on English teachers who, in spite of the curriculum controversy, were quietly enjoying the opportunities provided by GCSE to teach syllabuses which were examined entirely by coursework. He announced without warning that the amount of coursework in GCSE was too extensive and should be cut. The strictures applied to all subjects, but English teachers, who were passionate advocates of coursework, were the most wounded by Major's speech. A few months later the call for a revision of the English National Curriculum Order, referred to above, compounded the sense of injustice among English teachers.

Meanwhile, preparations had been going on at SEAC for the English tests at Key Stage 3. During the summer of 1992, while maths and science had a full-scale pilot involving 80 per cent of secondary schools, the English tests were piloted rather unsatisfactorily in a relatively small number of schools. The contract for developing them was taken from one group and given to another, but time was running out, as the compulsory Key Stage 3 English tests were due, along with maths and science, to be implemented in the summer of 1993. English teachers justifiably took the view that they ought to be informed at the start of the school year what form the testing might take at the end of it. In fact, the new contractors had not even piloted the tests by then. Worse still, John Patten, now the Secretary of State for Education, had just announced that a test on one of three specified Shakespeare plays would be compulsory. While, in principle, there was nothing wrong with testing 14-year olds in Shakespeare, the late decision was evidence of the haphazard state into which policy-making had descended. At a practical level, schools whose budget decisions would broadly have been made now had to stock up with one of John Patten's chosen texts. Once again, the way a decision was taken was blatantly humiliating. In the autumn, as various snippets of information emerged about the proposed English tests, a head of steam built up in the English teaching fraternity in favour of a test boycott. For the National Association of Teachers of English, and especially its London branch, this was their finest hour. Letters supporting a boycott began to arrive at NUT and other union headquarters, first in a trickle, then in a flood. There were, of course, politically extreme teachers keen to exploit the emerging opportunity. At NUT headquarters, officials were well versed in how to ignore the standard activists' protest; the campaign on the English tests was evidently different: both wider and deeper.

A routine meeting of the NUT Executive was due to take place on 9 and 10 December 1992. Following discussions at headquarters, the Executive unanimously carried a motion proposing an indicative ballot of English teachers to take place in January 1993. It would ask English teachers whether they would be prepared to boycott the tests in the summer, and other teachers whether they would take action in support of any English teachers who were disciplined for boycotting tests. With this motion approved, the NUT urged the Secretary of State to defer compulsory English tests and hold instead a non-statutory pilot, like those held for maths and science in 1992. It requested a meeting with the Secretary of State and publicized both to members and the public its criticisms of the proposed tests. They were poorly designed, lacked serious support, had not allowed schools to prepare properly and were being implemented during a review of the English National Curriculum which the government itself had instituted. John Patten turned down the meeting. This was hardly surprising. At the beginning of January 1993 he turned down an invitation to attend the North of England Education Conference, an event at which his predecessors for a generation had always made a set-piece speech. His reason was that he wanted instead to be interviewed on the Jimmy Young show. Lord Griffiths, in one of the more bizarre statements by a public official, described the tests as the best prepared in the history of education. Clearly, neither realized that they were staring into the abyss but, if the truth were told, neither did officials at union headquarters. There were some officials at NUT headquarters who doubted whether a majority of English teachers would support a test boycott: educational politics were entering uncharted waters.

When the result of the indicative ballot emerged towards the end of January, over 90 per cent of all those who responded said they would support a boycott. As the various ballots unfolded over the next two years, a pattern emerged. Members voted overwhelmingly for whatever the Executive recommended. In January 1993, however, this pattern had not become clear. The result was spectacular and, armed with it, the union stepped up the pressure. Responding to the ballot result, John Patten argued that the tests were sound and had been 'tried out in hundreds of schools in the past two and a half years'. Patten may have believed this; if so, he had been given inadequate briefing by Lord Griffiths and his colleagues at SEAC. In a letter to Patten, Doug McAvoy, General Secretary of the NUT, set out, step by step, how the crisis had arisen:

> The 1993 tests are based on pre-trial testing in 32 schools amongst pupils aged 15. The new board ... has had only nine months to devise the test. The materials on which the test of prior reading will be based arrived in schools at the beginning of February ... teachers are expected to cover a wide range of new literary material in less than the equivalent of one term, in addition to teaching the rest of the English curriculum. (Public letter to John Patten from Doug McAvoy, 1993)

The NUT's press release was less polite. Doug McAvoy said:

> In the face of united opposition to these English tests the Government's response is to try to rubbish its critics. That is the act of a desperate administration. Instead of facing up to reality, it suggests that the heads of independent schools, state schools, English teachers en masse and educationists are the dupes of a politically motivated group. That just makes the government look foolish ... By ignoring professional advice and parental concerns, the Government has built a monstrosity on a catalogue of incompetence. (NUT Press Release, 1993)

Somehow the mixed metaphor in a dispute about English seems exactly appropriate. At the same time, Doug McAvoy wrote to all chairs of governing bodies and to all headteachers, explaining the union's case. Here, he was kicking at an open door. All the unions had long since realized the importance of this target audience, who in any case were increasingly appalled at the performance of ministers.

I have concentrated on developments within the NUT during those crucial three months because the indicative ballot was a vital bold step. Nevertheless, as Sheila Dainton points out below, the ATL and, indeed, all the unions were campaigning vigorously on similar issues. Increasingly, too, they were unanimous in their condemnation not only of the government's policy on curriculum and assessment, but also of its whole approach to policy-making. Their members were overworked, demoralized and beginning to scream. To use a term from political science, teachers were rapidly being driven over the borders of the zone of indifference.

A joint statement from all six unions, condemning the English tests and urging the Secretary of State to turn them into a voluntary pilot, brought the crisis to a new peak. The Secretary of State finally agreed to meet leaders from each of the teachers' unions in mid-February. Since, by that time, he had turned down more than a dozen requests from the NUT for a meeting, this represented some progress, but not much. Each of the unions duly put the case in their varied ways but at this stage appeared to have had little impact. In any case, the phase of the saga in which the English tests were the central issue was drawing to a close. The prospect of a general test boycott was becoming a genuine possibility for the first time in history.

The test boycott

Competition between the six teachers' unions for members is fierce. It is the one genuine free market in education. No sooner had the NUT played its ace, than its fiercest rival, the National Association of Schoolmasters and Union of Women Teachers (NASUWT), came up with trumps. The NASUWT argued that a boycott would only be legal if it was a proper trade dispute and that it could only be a trade dispute if it was justified on the grounds of workload. They therefore argued that the NUT was wrong on two counts. Firstly, the issue of the dispute should not be whether the tests were educationally sound but whether they created unreasonable workload. Secondly, if that was the premise, then the boycott should not be just of the English tests but of all tests. They therefore balloted all their members, recommending that they support a boycott of all tests on the grounds of workload. At the time the other teachers' unions poured scorn, at least privately, on this step, and the government refused to meet the NASUWT. When the result emerged, however, there was a two-thirds majority in favour of a boycott. The NASUWT had learned from the NUT ballot that teachers were angry enough to take action; now they had showed it was true even among those such as maths teachers and primary school teachers who, less than a year earlier, had implemented tests with barely a grumble. The government's mishandling of the English issue had brought the whole house of cards tumbling down. Soon after the NASUWT boycott began, the union found itself in court. Wandsworth LEA, one of the Conservative's flagship councils, challenged the legality of their action, but the court found in the union's favour. This opened the floodgates.

All the other unions now found themselves under membership pressure to back the NASUWT boycott. The Easter Conference season was rapidly approaching and the government showed no signs of conceding. On 3 March the government announced that Sir Ron Dearing would chair the School Curriculum and Assessment Authority (SCAA) which in that September would replace the NCC and SEAC. In the meantime he would chair both the existing councils. This was a welcome surprise for teachers' union leaders. Dearing was known to be both honourable and pragmatic. It had been expected, not least by the man himself, that David Pascall, Chair of the NCC, would take on this crucial new role. He claimed that Baroness Blatch, Patten's deputy, had promised it to him. Although he had performed his role with honour, he had too much ideological baggage, lacked independence and had insufficient negotiating skills to do what Dearing eventually did.

Dearing's appointment was said to be due to the sage influence of Sir Geoffrey Holland, the new Permanent Secretary at the DFE. Taking up the post in January 1993 as the crisis gathered, Holland must have been wondering what he had let himself in for. If he was indeed responsible for Dearing's appointment, it was one of two highly significant achievements during his brief tenure. After a year in which he was frustrated by John Patten's apparent permanence as the crisis mounted, he took a post as Vice-Chancellor of Exeter University, leaving behind him not only Dearing, but also an organizational review of the DFE, the benefits of which were reaped by his successor.

It remained to be seen in March precisely what Sir Ron would be asked to do. John Patten was due to address the ATL Conference at the beginning of April, the first of three teachers' union conferences over the Easter holidays (see Sheila Dainton's account below for details). Whereas in January he could have saved the testing programme by making the English tests at Key Stage 3 optional, this would no longer suffice. A general boycott of all tests loomed. Even the traditionally moderate ATL was set to vote for a boycott. In the event, Patten made no concession at all on the tests, insisting that they go ahead. He did, however, announce a full-scale review of the National Curriculum, which Sir Ron would be asked to undertake in the summer term. In relation to long-standing union demands about the National Curriculum, this was a major concession. It was an acceptance that the curriculum was over-prescriptive and unmanageable. It was also a recognition that the policy process had been deeply flawed and that consultation had been noticeable only by its absence. However, it did nothing at all to relieve the workload on teachers in the short term. Not only that, it left the absurd English tests in place. As a result, it did nothing to alleviate the looming boycott. It is standard practice in negotiation to sacrifice short-term interests to gain long-term benefits. John Patten tried to do the reverse – which for obvious reasons is rare – and still failed.

Paradoxically, Patten's proposed review gave a generalized boycott even greater justification. What, after all, was the point of insisting on a set of tests based on a curriculum which the government had now accepted was unmanageable and in need of review? Early in the summer term ATL and NUT members voted overwhelmingly to join NASUWT members in a generalized boycott of all tests. Meanwhile, Wandsworth's appeal failed in the law courts, leaving Nigel de Gruchy, the NASUWT General Secretary, beaming. Then everyone stopped talking about the boycott. The unions issued advice. There was talk of possible punitive action taken by governors and LEAs, but in the event there was none – both groups were tacit supporters of the boycott. The government had rarely had fewer friends. Opinion polls even suggested that about 70 per cent of parents supported the teachers. Meanwhile, teaching went on; the tests were left in their packets; the boycott simply happened. It all seemed so easy. In spite of this complete humiliation, John Patten was not removed in the Prime Minister's summer re-shuffle. He did, however, disappear from the scene, temporarily suffering, not surprisingly, from a serious illness.

'A Framework for Reviewing the National Curriculum'

As the testing crisis had deepened, the teachers' organizations had been collaborating in the preparation of a document entitled 'A Framework for Reviewing the National Curriculum'. This idea had been proposed by the NUT to the 1992 summer conference that NCC had held for representatives of the teacher organizations. The first draft was prepared by the NUT and it was refined at a series of meetings during the autumn of 1992 (see Sheila Dainton's account below for further details). In December it was discussed with Chris Woodhead, then Chief Executive of NCC (who was consistently constructive during this period), and further refined for presentation to the NCC Council in early 1993. The gathering storm over testing, however, pushed it into the background temporarily. Nevertheless, by the time Sir Ron Dearing was appointed to review the National Curriculum the document had the support not only of the six unions, but also of six associations which represented independent schools. This was unprecedented. In his first full week at work on the curriculum Sir Ron Dearing received a copy of the document. The unions also distributed it to their branches, which were asked to ensure that it influenced as far as possible those members involved in the consultation exercise which took place during the summer of 1993. The document therefore had a double influence and its fingerprints can be found throughout the interim Dearing Report which was published at the beginning of August 1993. Backed as it was by the test boycott of that summer, it was one of the most influential teachers' union publications since the war.

The need to review the National Curriculum had been accepted by the NCC in the autumn of 1992. David Pascall, its Chairman, had said in a speech to Cambridgeshire headteachers that term: 'The more the NCC has listened to teachers talk about their work the more convinced we have become that the concerns are not just teething problems inevitable in a period of transition' (Pascall, 1992). At that stage, however, the NCC was still hooked on the idea that a subject-by-subject revision over the next few years would be sufficient to iron out the problems. It was reluctant to take the risk of a full-scale revision of the whole curriculum, the shorthand for which rapidly became 'the Big Bang'.

The teachers' unions' framework document came down firmly in favour of the Big Bang in spite of the fact that this would bring yet more disruption to members who, understandably, complained about an overload of change. It did so because the evidence pointed powerfully to structural flaws which a subject-by-subject revision would be unable to address. These flaws were most acute in Key Stage 2. Sir Ron's appointment to review the whole curriculum represented a recognition by John Patten of the case for a Big Bang. Nevertheless, during the summer Dearing considered various models, including an initial review of the core subjects first with a follow-up look at the others, before deciding in favour of the Big Bang approach in one overall review to take place during 1994 for implementation in 1995. That he had the courage to do so – in spite of the uncertainty it would cause for every teacher – owes a great deal to the joint commitment of the unions to a thoroughgoing approach. The unions' document argued that there was a need for a coherent overall view of the curriculum: 'If, as appears to be almost universally accepted, the foundation subjects of the NC in their current form take up too much time to allow for a balanced and broadly based curriculum, then there is clearly a need to reduce the extent of prescribed content' (Six Unions (SU), 1993, p. 4).

It then set out in broad terms what should be the content of a revised National Curriculum:

> The nationally defined curriculum must give the highest possible priority to the basics. These include literacy, numeracy and other aspects of communication. It follows therefore that – especially in Key Stage 1 – the highest priority must be given to reading, writing and basic computation ... It should be recognised, however, that these skills do not, by themselves, constitute an adequate definition of 'the basics'. The impact of half a century of unprecedented change on the learning needs of young people must be recognised. For example, IT competence must be considered a basic ... It follows that the basics should not be confused with the core subjects ...' (SU, 1993, p. 4).

This argument had implications for the process by which the curriculum should be reviewed:

A sensible approach to the whole curriculum, which should precede
further subject revision, would therefore be to achieve agreement about
what – across all ten foundation subjects – constitutes the basics. It is
essential that there should be a whole curriculum committee to look at
the relationships between the various components of the foundation
subjects. It would also be necessary to recognise the different needs of
children and young people at the different key stages. We would
suggest that there should be a committee for each of the four Key
Stages ... their conclusions ... could then inform the subject revisions. (SU, 1993, p. 5)

Broadly, this is what Dearing recommended. A committee made up of
NCC and SEAC members (before NCC and SEAC were merged to
form SCAA in September 1993) was formed to assist him. Then, in
1994, SCAA established Key Stage committees which ensured that the
different subject revisions did not come up with proposals which, taken
together, were unmanageable. As Chris Woodhead points out in his chapter below, these Key Stage committees took precedence over the subject
groups during the 1994 revision. Other recommendations from the
teachers' unions – in this document and others – on the process of a
review were also adopted by Dearing. Classroom teachers and heads
were involved in all the working groups; there was a series of well-attended
consultation conferences across the country; there were regular meetings with teachers' union representatives, monthly rather than termly,
during the critical period of decision-making between the summer of
1993 and the following spring. Indeed, by 1994 one union official told
me that he was, for the first time, suffering from 'consultation fatigue'.

   For those of us involved, the process was both exhilarating and almost
literally incredible. After years of chipping away, of being rebuffed, of
celebrating marginal successes, suddenly the policy gates had been flung
– or pushed – wide open and we were driving the agenda. There may well
be a generalizable policy lesson here. The generally held view of policy
development as an incremental process is by no means always accurate.
In times of conflict and uncertainty, it may be more likely to follow this
stop-start pattern. The key, in my view, to exploiting the fleeting periods
when the agenda is open is to know where you want to take it. As much
by luck as by judgement, the unions had arrived at an agreed agenda for
curriculum change in April 1993 at what turned out to be precisely the
right moment. Hence their huge influence over Dearing's curriculum
revision. Though the unions' document dealt with assessment, it was at
a much less specific level, and beneath the surface there were deep divisions on the issue. These became apparent in late 1993 and explain why
the unions have had less success in shaping the testing agenda following
the overwhelming success of the united test boycott that summer. Following the interim Dearing report of August 1993, the fragile unity in

the profession fell apart and, as a result, the unions lost control of the initiative.

Dearing and after

Sir Ron Dearing's interim report emerged, like many other curriculum documents before it, at the beginning of the school summer holidays. In this case there were no complaints about the timing, partly because everyone recognized that Dearing had made extraordinary progress in the space of four months, and partly because much of the message was welcome. Dearing's interim recommendations are published in Appendix I. The report set out a timetable for a Big Bang review of the National Curriculum and made proposals for a greatly reduced national testing programme confined to the basics. It also urged that teacher assessment be given equal weight with tests in terms of reporting to parents. Though the report proposed to maintain the ten-level scale for the time being, it wisely confirmed that GCSE would continue to use the grading system put in place when it had been established in 1986. Here was the basis of a new curriculum settlement in which the 5–14 curriculum would be seen as separate from and preparation for a coherent 14–19 curriculum. The latter half of this settlement remains to be achieved, though Sir Ron Dearing has been asked to review post-16 qualifications in 1995 and will no doubt have this in mind as an ultimate goal. Significant though these proposals were, in some ways more important was the approach Dearing had taken to arriving at his conclusions and the tone in which his interim report was written. Given that the flaws in the policy process had been responsible for the breakdown, putting it back on an even keel was a crucial part of the solution.

Throughout the summer, in spite of the test boycott (which Dearing wisely avoided mentioning whenever possible), he and his extremely hard-working staff organized a series of consultation conferences around the country. Through the TES they urged teachers to write to them. Meanwhile, a series of meetings took place, both with all the teachers' organizations together, and with each one separately. Following the developments of the previous twelve months, the curriculum and testing had become the highest priority issue for unions, and the general secretaries were now wheeled in, well-briefed and ready for the fray. One of their key roles was the presentation of the conflict on the media and, in my view, collectively they came over excellently. Given that John Patten, and for much of the early part of the year, Brian Griffiths spoke for the rival point of view, they were batting on an easy wicket. Dearing charmed all his audiences with a mix of avuncular common sense and a shrewd ability to spot both the building blocks of consensus and the weaknesses in the positions of others. These conferences were different from any that had come before. Dearing or Chris Woodhead or Hilary Nicolle, the Chief

Executives of NCC and SEAC respectively, opened the proceedings by setting out what the issues were, after which small working groups sought solutions. Staff from NCC or SEAC chaired the meetings and took notes, which were later circulated for participants to check that their views had been recorded accurately. Simple, open gestures such as this – unheard of in the madness of the previous year – made a major contribution to changing the climate.

At the meetings between the six unions and Sir Ron Dearing the atmosphere became more tense, not because of Sir Ron, but because of the rivalry among the six general secretaries who were now involved. Nevertheless, by sticking closely to the common ground and avoiding divisive issues such as whether external markers would be a good idea, the meetings proved broadly effective. I had the task of presenting the common case on behalf of the six, and found that, with the aid of a few phone calls beforehand and a brief pre-meeting, it was possible to establish and maintain a common position.

In the summer conference for the teachers' unions at the NCC that year, we presented to Sir Ron our views on how the relationship between the SCAA (due to replace NCC and SEAC that September) and the teachers' unions could be put on a firmer footing. Our paper is worth quoting at length both because its broad thrust was accepted and implemented by Sir Ron, and because the moderation of its demands demonstrates how utterly flawed the policy process had been prior to 1993. It set out nine principles on which the relationship should be founded. These were as follows:

(i) Teachers are not simply a workforce required to implement the National Curriculum, but a professional group whose views should be taken into account in the policy-making process.

(ii) The teacher organisations are genuinely representative of the views of the teaching profession, and therefore centrally important to the policy-making and implementation process.

(iii) It should not be assumed that policy will be initiated solely by central government. Ideas for improvement in curriculum and assessment should be expected from all levels in the service.

(iv) All policy ideas, whatever the origin, should be refined through consultation of relevant parties, including teachers and their organisations, prior to implementation.

(v) As far as possible, it should be recognised that change can be more easily implemented where it is planned and predictable, rather than haphazard and opportunist.

(vi) During the implementation process, it is essential that those responsible for policy, including ministers, receive accurate and balanced feedback and that systems are established to ensure that this happens.

(vii) The effects, or likely effects, of a given set of proposals on pupil achievement should be an important criterion in deciding how to proceed. For this reason, research evidence should be given high status.

(viii) All data on which decisions are based should be open to public scrutiny.

(ix) The new SCAA needs to take seriously, and base its modus operandi upon, the important statement of its new Chair, that he is accountable not only to the Secretary of State, but also to the whole community of parents, pupils and teachers.

On 21 July 1993 the six unions met Sir Ron Dearing for the final time before he submitted his report to ministers and reinforced their joint position. The paper for the meeting finished with the only partly serious assertion that: 'However good the messenger is, s/he will probably get shot if the message is absurd' (union paper in possession of the author, 1993). The inclusion of this sentence is, in fact, evidence of how much relations had already been improved. Dearing's evident goodwill made all the difference.

The tone of Dearing's interim report provided further evidence that this was a new era. One quotation from his covering letter to John Patten, which went with the report, will suffice:

> Anyone coming new to an assignment like this needs to take some bearings. In doing so I have been deeply impressed – at times moved – by the strong commitment of everyone concerned in education to serve our children well. What is equally clear is that standards of educational achievement need to rise if our children are to lead fulfilling lives in the 21st century and, as a nation, we are to thrive in an increasingly competitive world. The National Curriculum and its assessment arrangements were introduced as the key initiative in the drive to raise standards. I am clear that these policy initiatives were well-conceived and are beginning to produce results. We need, nevertheless, to learn some hard lessons from the early years of implementing the National Curriculum – there are some very real issues which we must address to help teachers in their task.
>
> In the light of my consultations over three months, I have not hesitated to make broad recommendations for action where there is a well-founded basis for change and where I think there is a wide measure of support for it. (SCAA, 1993, p. 1)

Following the interim Dearing Report, the issue for the unions was whether they should lift the workload sanctions that had been the backbone of the test boycott. In the event, none of them did. Though Dearing's report had pointed the way to solutions of the curriculum problems and made some progress, from the teachers' point of view, on testing, few of its provisions made any appreciable difference to the immediate workload pressures on teachers. Moreover, there was a number of major issues on which Dearing had decided to consult further during the autumn. It was felt by most teachers' leaders that in these circumstances it was best to keep the pressure on. There were also those who believed that the Dearing Report was simply a new gloss on the same government policy; among those who argued this were the minority of teachers who were wholeheartedly opposed both to a national curriculum and to national assessment.

My own view at the time, which I am sure was a minority view, was that the underlying issue was the policy process. Since Dearing had demonstrated that this was being repaired and had, in terms of the major curriculum demands, accepted almost all that the unions had asked for, I thought that the boycott should have been lifted, or allowed to fade out, as a gesture of good will. The events of the previous summer had demonstrated, after all, that the boycott could have been reimposed if the process spiralled out of control once more. This, however, seemed unlikely. During John Patten's long summer absence through illness, a new atmosphere of realism had broken out. The DFE had been left in the capable hands of Baroness Blatch and the increasingly assertive Permanent Secretary, Geoffrey Holland. All the unions had been invited to meet ministers to discuss an agenda of their choosing in the summer and were invited to return in September.

Meanwhile, SCAA had been launched, with Chris Woodhead as its decisive Chief Executive and Sir Ron Dearing as its Chairman. It, too, went about its business with an air of openness and realism as it tried consciously (and successfully) to put the old cloak-and-dagger atmosphere behind it. It proceeded to consult on the remaining critical issues with the same thoroughness which had characterized its approach the previous term.

The major issues still out for consultation were the shape of the curriculum at Key Stage 4, the timetable for slimming down the curriculum (and particularly whether revised subject Orders should be implemented simultaneously or over a period of time), whether the ten-level scale should be retained or replaced and the amount of time that the prescribed curriculum should occupy at each key stage. Dearing also acknowledged that, in his interim report, he had failed to give sufficient thought to the question of special educational needs, and that he wanted to redress this in his final report.

This was published early in January 1994. A summary of its main conclusions and recommendations are published in Appendix II. The central recommendation appears at the start of its second section:

The National Curriculum is fundamental to raising educational standards. Urgent action is needed to reduce the statutorily required content of its programmes of study and to make it less prescriptive and less complex. A closely co-ordinated review of all the statutory curriculum Orders should immediately be put in hand, guided by the need to:

(i)   reduce the volume of material required by law to be taught;
(ii) simplify and clarify the programmes of study;
(iii) reduce prescription so as to give more scope for professional judgement;
(iv) ensure that the Orders are written in a way which offers maximum support to the classroom teachers. (SCAA, 1994, p. 7)

Meanwhile, other advice that had been sent out during the autumn on the subject of recording and reporting assessment had offered demonstrable reductions in workload. The testing arrangements for the summer of 1994, which by this stage were well on their way to development, had also clearly offered significant reductions in workload. While their educational merit remained open to question, the new open policy process offered the opportunity for them to be evaluated and refined over time.

By this time I had left the NUT and, writing immediately after the publication of the final Dearing Report, concluded that:

Sir Ron Dearing's final report, published last week, presents both the teacher unions and the government with a moment of truth. Sir Ron, a pragmatist to the core, has not produced the perfect national curriculum but he has set out a workable compromise ...

The government has had the courage to accept the report in full. It should now demonstrate, through its actions in the months ahead, its commitment to the Dearing settlement ...

From the teaching profession's point of view, the first response should be one of celebration. Last May the six teacher unions jointly submitted proposals for revision of the National Curriculum and its assessment. They urged reduced prescription, reduced teacher workload, the provision of greater room for the exercise of professional judgement, a simplified curriculum structure, fewer tests and professional involvement in decision-making. They also suggest that once these new arrangements were in place there should be no further change to it for five years.

Sir Ron has delivered in every case.

No doubt teachers will have continuing doubts. They will remain concerned about the nature of the national tests, though everyone agrees they are much more sensible this year than last. They will also worry about the government's continued insistence on school-by-school league tables of the test results of 11 and 16 year olds. And underlying all of this, many teachers are still deeply suspicious of government education policy and sceptical about the competence of ministers. Union leaderships will inevitably reflect these concerns of their members. Indeed some may take the view that they justify a continued boycott of the tests. However tempting, these siren voices must be ignored. Teachers have not won everything they wanted from the 1993 conflict, but they have won far more than anyone might have dreamed a year ago.

For unions, in education as well as other industries, the most difficult decision always is when to settle. They have after all to work hard to encourage the membership to take action. This involves magnifying the cause and making sure the opposition is pilloried. Suddenly, if the union settles, the membership no doubt with remaining anxieties, as in the case of teachers, is told, that normal service should be resumed. In these circumstances courageous leadership is required. Given the likelihood of flak from the membership, continuing the action is often the easier option. But genius, as Goethe said, is knowing when to stop. For the teaching profession this is the moment. Now Dearing has produced his carefully constructed proposals, the overwhelming priority for the nation should be raising standards for all pupils. To use the words Sir Ron used at the press launch of his report, pupils and teachers must be switched on. That surely is what parents and the public in general will want to see.

They will not understand if the tests are boycotted this summer. They would find it extraordinary to see a boycott proceeding after Sir Ron Dearing has given teachers virtually everything they asked for. They would then be forced to conclude that the real motive for a boycott was not to improve the National Curriculum and its testing arrangements, but a gut opposition to all tests and a fearful defensiveness about accountability. A 1994 boycott could not therefore gain the kind of public support that the 1993 boycott generated. On the contrary, it would separate teachers from their most important allies, parents.

Instead, the teacher unions should recognise that the counterpart of last year's success is responsibility. They should make the most of the new opportunities that involvement in the policy process brings. They could also begin to urge government to apply the Dearing approach – listening, consultation and pragmatism – to other aspects of education policy. If teacher unions are to succeed in the next decade they must be seen to be promoting higher standards, not standing in the way of them. This will not always be easy. Responsibility never is. It means for example making constructive contributions to the two most crucial debates facing education. If teachers believe the government's league tables are an unsatisfactory means of holding schools accountable, what do they believe would work better? And how best can schools, especially those in urban areas, be enabled to raise standards dramatically

before the turn of the century? Dearing has played his part magnif-
icently. The teacher unions must choose between responsibility and
oblivion. (Barber, 1994b)

There is excessive hype in what I wrote, but the gist of my argument
still stands. All the unions but one followed the final Dearing report by
calling off their boycott.

Only the NUT stood out; it certainly had a case. The tests remained
of doubtful validity. They were still linked to performance tables at 16
and perhaps at 11 to which teachers were hostile and, in spite of the
Dearing promises, no one could say for certain how much the workload
would actually fall. More importantly, it was evident that many teachers
were deeply suspicious of government in general and of its policy on
curriculum and assessment in particular. Given what had happened in
the last six years, it was hardly surprising that the spirit of forgiveness
was in limited supply. In addition, therefore, to the arguments of principle, there was a potential membership advantage in continuing the
boycott after other unions had called it off. Furthermore, John Patten
remained Secretary of State. He was deeply despised and had an
ingrained habit of blundering. The previous autumn he had caused outrage by describing one of the country's most respected educationists,
Tim Brighouse, as 'a nutter'. Most of the profession believed that John
Major should have sacked him in the July 1993 reshuffle. So – rumour
had it – did Geoffrey Holland, the Permanent Secretary at the DFE.
Teachers' leaders – not only those in the NUT – were of the view that
it would be difficult, perhaps impossible, to trust him and that therefore
the Dearing settlement could not necessarily be relied upon. This,
and the pressure from the union's left-wing activists, added up to a substantial case for a continued boycott.

The NUT boycott of 1994 was sufficiently effective to disrupt the
testing programme, but not powerful enough, without the support of
the other unions, to put a more constructive alternative in place. It also
encouraged the government to make concessions to those unions that had
effectively settled. At the 1994 Easter conferences Baroness Blatch
charmed both the ATL and NASUWT leaderships. More importantly,
the government conceded the NASUWT's demand for the external marking of Key Stage 2 and 3 tests. This made a significant contribution to
reducing workload, but only at a cost of £30 million, which could otherwise have been invested in the improvement of teachers' assessment skills.

In the summer of 1994 John Patten was finally removed from office,
shortly after conceding to Tim Brighouse's libel case. He was replaced
by the emollient and effective Gillian Shephard. At about the same time
Doug McAvoy secured his own re-election as General Secretary of
the NUT. The way to a final settlement was beginning to open up. It
was increasingly clear that the best the NUT could hope for was

continued stalemate until another election, when Labour might have let teachers off the hook.

Any notion that this was a realistic policy option was dispelled in the autumn of 1994 when Labour's new leader Tony Blair and new education spokesperson David Blunkett made it abundantly clear that standards, particularly in urban areas and for the disadvantaged, and the accountability of public services, were both high on New Labour's agenda. Although in the autumn term of 1994, NUT members, again following the Executive's recommendation, voted in favour of continuing the boycott into 1995, the union's leaders were seeking peace with honour. To their credit, they achieved it when the government promised a full scale evaluation of the 1995 tests and consultations about its implications. In early 1995 the Executive recommended that the boycott be lifted and the union's members duly backed the new moderate line. With the trustworthy Gillian Shephard in post, the policy process had at last arrived at equilibrium.

It remains to be seen whether the tests that were implemented smoothly in the summer of 1995 fulfil the direst predictions of their critics or the startling gains promised by their advocates. The truth is likely to lie somewhere in between. It also remains to be seen whether the Dearing curriculum, effective from September 1995, will work well. Still less clear is whether the performance tables will benefit education in either their present or any future refined form. On each of these, the evidence remains to be gathered and analysed.

Three things, however, are clear. Firstly, a new compromise has been reached on the issue of professional discretion. The pre-1988 autonomy has gone, and rightly so. The excessive and insulting prescription ushered in by Kenneth Baker has gone too. In place of both is Sir Ron Dearing's middle way: 'I recommend that ... the excessive prescription of the National Curriculum [must be] removed particularly outside the core subjects. This is a recognition that the professionalism of teachers must be trusted. Trust carries with it, however, the duty of accountability: the greater the trust, the clearer the accountability must be' (NCC, 1993, p. 10).

This was reinforced in the letter which Sir Ron sent to all heads with the revised Orders (distributed to schools in January 1995) urging that teachers use their professional judgement. Here was the seed of a new refined National Curriculum for the twenty-first century.

Secondly, the conflict over the National Curriculum has taught everyone some tough lessons about the policy process. The government, the DFE and the various quangos have learnt that it is dangerous, damaging and sometimes humiliating to run roughshod over the teaching profession. They have also learnt that ministers lose respect and that policy is brought into disrepute if it is changed on a whim. The teaching profession, meanwhile, has learnt that educational change is permanent, that the painfully slow old-fashioned partnership model has gone for good and that a focus on standards and improvement is important. They have also experienced both the power of unity and the weakness of division. Above all they have learnt that real strength, identified by the NUT as long ago as 1991, lies in close alliances with parents and governors at both national and school level. The alliances first established over testing are already proving their worth in relation to education funding.

Finally, out of all the conflict has emerged a new and exciting educational focus on school effectiveness and school improvement. The fact that the government announced its 'Improving Schools' initiative in the summer of 1995, shortly after the major curriculum and assessment issues had been settled, is not a coincidence. The settlement has provided a new, perhaps unique opportunity to build a crusade for school improvement and it is clear that both government and the buoyant opposition are gearing up to lead it.

Dearing, with government backing, has promised a five-year moratorium on curriculum change. This was demanded by the six unions in 1993 and conceded. It seems likely that, if Labour is elected in a General Election, it would adhere to the moratorium. We need to achieve in the year 2000 not a curriculum which is a workable compromise, but one truly worthy of a new millennium. The moral of the curriculum controversy is that it will not be achieved by spending another five years debating the curriculum, but by focusing on school improvement and rebuilding the triangular relationship between government, teachers and society. If all that is achieved in the next few years, establishing an excellent National Curriculum at the turn of the century will not be all that hard.

3
The National Curriculum and its Assessment

Chris Woodhead

Introduction

What follows is more personal reflection than dispassionate analysis. To a degree, this is inevitable. The National Curriculum is only seven years old. The consultation on the revision of the National Curriculum following the Dearing Review has only recently been converted, and, as a former Chief Executive of the School Curriculum and Assessment Authority (SCAA), I have my own individual perspective on things. But I must confess at the outset that I have not even attempted the balance of the judicious review. My aims in this essay are rather to identify some critical points of dispute about the need for and nature of the National Curriculum and to discuss these controversies in terms of the changes that I believe we must work for if we are to improve the quality of the education we offer our pupils. The essay is personal, therefore, in this more deliberate and radical sense. I shall deal first with the curriculum and then turn to assessment issues.

The curriculum

Why we need a National Curriculum

There are two reasons why we need a National Curriculum. First, while a balance must clearly be struck between local autonomy and central prescription, the situation prior to the introduction of the National Curriculum was unsatisfactory in that individual schools had a large measure of freedom to determine what they taught. Problems consequently arose when a child moved from one part of the country to another. But, more fundamentally, the fact that there was no nationally agreed statement about a common entitlement meant that in primary schools many children had no meaningful teaching in, say, science, history or geography, and at secondary level, for example, far too many girls were failing to follow courses in science through to the age of sixteen. The National Curriculum is a safeguard against unacceptable eccentricities in local provision. The second reason is that much depends on the expectations which a teacher has of his/her pupils. When everything was left to the judgement of the individual school, levels of expectation inevitably varied from one school to another. The National Curriculum is an attempt to define challenging but realistic expectations of what children should know, understand and be able to do as they move through school. It is a way of raising expectation and therefore standards of pupil achievement.

The views of teachers

The many meetings I have had with teachers over recent years to discuss their experience of implementing the National Curriculum have convinced me that the profession as a whole accepts the arguments outlined above and sees the National Curriculum as a good thing in principle. This is not to deny that there are concerns and disagreements. Most obviously, there is the conviction (discussed below) that the requirements of the pre-Dearing programmes of study were difficult, if not impossible, to cover in the teaching time available. But, while problems of overload are of great importance, they are second-order issues. There are more fundamental points of dispute – such as the alleged lack of a philosophical rationale, the subject structure at primary level, decisions taken on individual subjects, and the process by which the curriculum was defined and introduced – which need to be discussed before I turn to problems of overload and the decisions of the Dearing Report.

A lack of rationale?

Those (like Philip O'Hear and John White) who argue that the National Curriculum is fundamentally flawed because it lacks any underpinning rationale, believe that the details of the programmes of study should flow inexorably from some general statement about the purposes of education. The first difficulty I have with this viewpoint is that statements of educational purpose are usually so generalized and pious that one can do no more than nod sagely and pass on by. O'Hear and White talk, for example, about equipping young people to function effectively in a liberal-democratic society. What do phrases like this really mean? Is it possible to trace the details of what should be taught back to such aims? Would the resulting curriculum requirements actually differ from those which we have at present? The answer to these questions is, at least in O'Hear's and White's case, no. Their curriculum involves some language study, some mathematics, some science, and so on. The *post hoc* justification of these areas of learning might make us feel more comfortable about the existing National Curriculum, but it hardly amounts to a convincing attack on current arrangements.

A curriculum which is organized in terms of different subjects can be defended satisfactorily against accusations that it is an ill-considered throwback to the grammar school curriculum of the 1950s. Human beings have, over the years, come to organize their understanding of the world in different ways. Science is, for example, different from history. And education ought to be concerned with the initiation of young people into these different forms of human understanding. This is justification enough for the subject structure of the National Curriculum.

Knowledge versus skills

But why, some ask, do we continue to be satisfied by arguments which are premised on the belief that education is an activity which can be justified in terms of its own intrinsic worth? The CBI and others who promote the importance of generic skills (communication, numeracy, problem-solving and so on) come close to questioning the point of spending time on the 'academic' and therefore 'irrelevant' content of the National Curriculum subjects. Employers are interested, we are told, in those who are competent in these essential skills, not those who are knowledgeable in and enthusiastic about, say, literature or history. The answer to such critics is that, while the National Curriculum must most certainly be an adequate preparation for the world of employment, it must also be defensible on grounds that go beyond the strictly utilitarian. It must, that is, constitute an adequate initiation into the cultural, moral and intellectual understandings to which the 1988 Act refers. Such understanding is the bedrock upon which more specific training can later be built. But we need not and should not see this issue as an either/or. It is, as a point of pedagogic fact, impossible to conceive of a curriculum which seeks to develop skills in a context which is content-free. The question, therefore, is 'What content are we to teach?' The approach in the National Curriculum is to define content that is worthwhile in the sense that it encapsulates the knowledge and understanding which is essential to a basic grasp of the key disciplines. The Orders also identify essential skills within each subject and, collectively, they offer pupils the chance to develop their competence in the basic skills of literacy and numeracy. They fulfil both aims.

Subjects and the Primary Curriculum

The criticism that the National Curriculum is irrelevant to the world of business and industry tends, for obvious reasons, to be levelled most sharply at Key Stages 3 and 4. At Key Stages 1 and 2, the concern is rather that an approach which defines what has to be taught in terms of individual subjects is inappropriate for primary-age children. In one sense, this is not a real issue. It is for the individual school to decide how the curriculum is to be organized. The decision may be to teach some or even all of the National Curriculum requirements as separate subjects. But, equally, it may be to integrate these requirements. In so far as the success of any integrated or thematic approach depends upon the clarity with which the elements to be integrated are defined, then the advent of the National Curriculum ought to improve the quality of thematic teaching. Schools should not see the National Curriculum as a threat to integration.

It would, however, be disingenuous to pretend that the introduction of the National Curriculum has not fuelled the debate within primary education about separate subject teaching. It is quite clear that the majority of primary schools are now working carefully from the programmes of study, and planning the curriculum very much more systematically than they did in the past. This is a very important step forward. Despite laments about a loss of spontaneity, this more rigorous planning must help to ensure a more balanced, coherent range of educational experience for the child. And, beyond this, many primary schools are thinking hard about which National Curriculum subjects (or elements within subjects) are taught most effectively as discrete units. We shall no doubt continue to see some degree of subject integration for the foreseeable future. Effective schools will continue to co-ordinate the teaching of basic skills across the curriculum. But I am convinced that more systematic planning, a greater use of separate subject teaching, and, in larger schools, a greater use of specialist subject teachers will lead to the requirements of the National Curriculum being met more effectively and to a raising of standards. If, therefore, the introduction of the National Curriculum amounts to a challenge to conventional assumptions about primary education, it is a challenge which is being met, and met positively, in many schools.

Disputes over subjects: who should define the National Curriculum?

Turning to individual subjects, the initial definition of what had to be taught went remarkably smoothly, given the potential for conflict. Some pigeons have only subsequently come home to roost. There was an underlying conflict (touched on above) between those who believed that the curriculum should focus on skills and processes, and those who wanted to give greater weight to specific subject knowledge. This apart, the difficulties were relatively minor. In history, for example, some commentators expressed their concerns about a lack of emphasis on British history, and others argued that the Order encouraged teachers to stimulate the vagaries of empathetic understanding, rather than to concentrate upon hard facts. Such controversies were, however, contained without too much difficulty, and, leaving aside problems of curriculum overload, the teaching profession as a whole did not find it hard to accept the original National Curriculum Orders as a reasonable encapsulation of what was deemed to be good practice.

Perhaps inevitably, the temperature has increased, as experience of teaching the Orders has built up. In most subjects, though, the controversies have continued to be fewer than might have been predicted. Whether this is a good or bad thing depends on whether you judge current practice in British classrooms to be of an acceptable standard. This is an important point because it raises the question whether the National Curriculum *ought* to be challenging conventional assumptions about how different subjects should be taught. One view, articulated by those who see any national curriculum as an imposition which erodes professional autonomy, is that the Orders ought to capture what teachers believe to be good practice. The other is that the introduction of the National Curriculum offers a unique opportunity to challenge conventional professional assumptions and to inject a dose of lay common sense into an area of public life which has for too long been insulated from external influence.

The clearest example of this dispute has been the English Order. By and large, English teachers liked the initial Cox curriculum. They liked its emphasis on writing for a range of purposes and audiences, the emphasis it placed on learning about language, the gentleness of its approach to the teaching of literature passed down from the great tradition. It was not surprising, therefore, that they greeted the National Curriculum Council Review of the English Order with some dismay. This essay is not the place to debate the particulars of this dismay. It is, rather, the constitutional point which I want to discuss. Whose curriculum, in the end, should it be? What constitutes a proper balance between the professional educationalists' view of what should be taught and the views of parents, governors, employers and politicians? This leads me to questions concerning the implementation of the National Curriculum.

I have talked to enough parents and employers to know that, outside the world of education, there are many who feel that standards of literacy are nowhere near high enough. It is not that standards have necessarily declined (though many think they have), but rather that, looking to the increasing demands of the twenty-first century, they must be raised. This in itself does not raise any constitutional difficulties, because most English teachers would agree. But public disquiet goes beyond a concern about standards to a scepticism about teaching priorities. Many employers, for example, think that the English Order should pay greater attention to the teaching of standard English so that youngsters can communicate confidently in situations which demand fluent and correct linguistic usage. They demand a mastery of the basic skills of spelling, punctuation and grammar, while many English teachers, whilst recognizing the importance of these skills, are determined not to lose an equal emphasis on teaching children to write for a range of purposes and audiences. There is, in short, a considerable difference of view between organizations like the National Association for the Teaching of English and many, if not most, parents and employers.

How should this conflict be resolved? I do not think that it is reasonable for the teaching profession to argue that the professional view must automatically prevail. If the government wants the National Curriculum to be implemented with professional support and full commitment, then it must pay careful attention to the views of teachers. If it decides to reject their views, it must have good reasons and evidence for so doing. But education is too important to the future of our society and too expensive in terms of the resources it consumes for the curriculum to be left entirely to the judgement of the profession. Those who disagree with this statement often argue that nobody would dream of telling a surgeon how to set about a complex operation and that it is unreasonable, on this analogy, for anyone other than teachers to have a view on what and how English or any other subject should be taught. While, however, the aims of surgery are uncontested, there is a great deal of disagreement about the purposes of English teaching. It is, moreover, not entirely true to say that lay people have no legitimate concern in medical procedures: some operations and medical objectives (such as lobotomies and genetic engineering) are the legitimate focus of a great deal of public interest. And the same is true, of course, of some teaching techniques – a teacher who believed that the most efficient way to inspire his/her children to love Shakespeare was to beat them would be roundly and rightly condemned by parents and teachers alike. If there is a clear-cut distinction to be made between the conduct of a brain operation and an English lesson, it is that the latter is inescapably shot through with a complex of value judgements. The operation, once begun, is a technical matter; the English lesson involves value judgements about content and process which depend upon prior assumptions about issues which are of fundamental interest to the state. It is because it is particularly difficult to separate the what from the how in English that it has proved to be the most controversial of all National Curriculum subjects. In principle, I do not think that the state should involve itself in matters of pedagogic technique. But, given that the state funds education and that many of its citizens are (rightly or wrongly) critical of what schools are achieving, I do not think anyone in education can simply raise the professional drawbridge.

I think, therefore, that the NUT is wrong or, at least, simplistic in its stance when it talks of an 'imposed' National Curriculum. The National

Curriculum has to be the product of a complex and lengthy set of discussions which involve all who have a stake in the future of the education service. It is the (often unenviable) job of the SCAA to listen to the range of views expressed on every National Curriculum subject, to weigh the different arguments, and to come to an independent judgement about the recommendations that it should make to the Secretary of State. Those who are critical of present arrangements often object not so much to the approach in principle as to what they see as political influence over the deliberations of bodies which the government has itself appointed. Having worked for four years within first the NCC and more recently the SCAA, I can say this: the individuals who take the decisions represent a wide spectrum of views. Each body has, of course, had members who are known for their particular beliefs. But there has never been an overall leaning in a particular direction. The complexity of discussion on most important issues makes a mockery of the simple political polarities and conspiracy theories beloved of educational commentators.

The problem of overload

At Key Stage 2, and to a lesser extent at Key Stages 1 and 3, teachers argued strongly throughout the Dearing Review that there is too much ground to cover. With the wisdom of hindsight, it is obvious that the NCC and the Department for Education ought to have exercised tighter control over the understandable enthusiasms of the subject groups who drew up the first subject Orders. The lesson has certainly been learnt by the SCAA and, throughout the recent review, the Key Stage Advisory Groups and SCAA's officers saw the overall key stage perspective as a dominant priority.

The judgements involved in slimming down curriculum content proved difficult for a number of reasons. In part, this was because different constituencies within the profession take different views on the nature and extent of the slimming required. The subject associations and teachers commenting on particular subjects were by and large content with the cuts made in the draft proposals. But those who take the overview, predictably, argued for greater reductions, in particular at Key Stage 2. The SCAA had to balance these and other conflicting arguments. More fundamentally, the difficulty was one of trying to determine how much time is needed to meet a particular curriculum objective. One can only rely here on the advice of a range of teachers. The SCAA has done this, recognizing that circumstances in individual schools will greatly affect the time which is actually involved. Judgements about the weight of curriculum content cannot be taken in a vacuum: the subject knowledge and understanding which the teacher possesses, and the rigour and effectiveness of the curriculum planning undertaken by the school, will have a material influence on what it is possible to teach. These considerations were particularly relevant at primary level, where the National Curriculum has posed the greatest challenge to current practice. The SCAA has had to walk something of a tightrope in order to avoid either falling into the trap of setting expectations which are unrealistically high, or failing to recognize that, as subject knowledge and planning improve, it will be possible to cover more ground than is currently the case in some primary schools. The aim in the SCAA has been to challenge, but to do so realistically. Equally, it has sought to reduce the curriculum to the knowledge, understanding and skill which it is essential to teach at each key stage. The drive to reduce stems first and foremost from the recognition that the current curriculum simply cannot be taught in the time available. But it is also rooted in the belief that there must be some room for the exercise of local discretion about what is taught. Schools serve different communities and need the flexibility to respond to the particular challenges they face and to make use of the special opportunities they possess. Teachers, too, ought to be able to utilize their individual expertise and enthusiasm. And, as Sir Ron Dearing has argued throughout the consultation and Review, teachers, like everyone else, are most likely to work with enthusiasm if they feel that they have control over their daily commitments.

It is worth emphasizing that the process of slimming down has involved more than a reduction in content: the SCAA has also made a determined effort to reduce prescription and to eliminate anything which constitutes a methodological steer. The original Orders are, in places, closer to being manuals on what is deemed to be effective teaching than clear, straightforward statements of the knowledge, understanding and skill that children should be taught. In the SCAA's view, the former approach is an unacceptable intrusion into what should be the professional decision of the individual teacher and school. If guidance of any kind is needed, then it should appear not in the statutory Order itself, but in documentation which accompanies but which is clearly separate from the Order. This minimalist approach ought to ensure that individual schools do have the freedom to teach the National Curriculum requirements in their own way and to supplement them with additional teaching which is built upon their particular expertise and designed to meet local needs. There will always be an argument as to how much time the National Curriculum should occupy. Those who object to any government intrusion into what are deemed to be strictly professional matters, and those whose general aspiration is to roll back the boundaries of state interference, will both argue for a National Curriculum which is yet further reduced. I have some sympathy with this. But my personal experience of education persuades me that, while there is a risk of the

Orders strait-jacketing the good school, the greater danger is that of reducing National Curriculum requirements too far and so turning the clock back to the eccentricity of local provision which characterized the service prior to 1988.

Assessment

The present situation

My guess is that the slimmed down National Curriculum, introduced in September 1995, will go a very long way to meeting teachers' concerns about curriculum overload. I am hopeful, therefore, that we can look forward to the five-year moratorium on further major change as a period in which schools can work positively to implement a National Curriculum which is accepted as both manageable and intellectually challenging.

The situation with regard to assessment is less clear. There is no consensus amongst either the teachers' associations or teachers themselves about many of the issues involved in the debate about assessment. The key issues are the interrelationship of the tests and teacher assessment within the overall assessment framework, the educational soundness of the tests, the workload implications, and the use of assessment data in the compilation of school performance tables. I shall discuss each of these issues in turn.

The overall assessment framework

Anyone who has ever taught knows that teacher assessment is at the heart of effective teaching. If teachers do not have a clear picture of what their pupils know, understand and can do, then they cannot match their learning to what has already been mastered. Diagnostic teacher assessment is a key element within effective classroom teaching. There is, similarly, broad agreement that teacher assessment should play an important part, alongside the National Curriculum tests, in the summative assessment of pupil achievement. This is because the tests cannot assess all aspects of the programmes of study. If we want a complete picture of what a pupil has mastered, then the teacher's assessment of the progress the pupil has made through the relevant key stage must be reported alongside the test result. The more contentious questions of what this might mean in terms of workload, and what it should mean in terms of external audit, are discussed below, but the principle appears to have general professional support. The tests may, for their part, contribute something to the teacher's understanding of his/her pupils' achievements, but their prime purpose is summative. They contribute an efficient means of providing parents with information about their children's progress in the core subjects of English and mathematics at Key Stage 1 and English, mathematics and science at Key Stages 2 and 3, measured against national norms at the end of these key stages.

It is sometimes said that parents do not want this information, and that, in any case, the bald statement of the level which the pupil has achieved is much less useful than the teacher's verbal comment. On the latter point, I do not see why it should be an either/or. Of course, the teacher's description of the pupil's strengths and weaknesses is potentially very useful. But so, too, is information which tells parents where their child is in terms of national norms. I can well believe that many parents are not yet showing much enthusiasm for the reporting of levels: any innovation takes a while to be understood, and much depends upon what the person who is doing the explaining feels about the worth of the initiative.

Are the tests educationally sound?

Some teachers argue the more fundamental point that the levels are worthless because the tests upon which they are based are unsound. The argument here is either that *all* tests are unsound (because, for example, it is thought that to write against the clock is an artificial exercise which subjects pupils to unacceptable pressure, or that no test can do justice to any curricular objectives), or that the National Curriculum tests do not constitute a valid assessment of the programmes of study of the National Curriculum Orders.

I have met few teachers who believe that all tests are unsound. Some Key Stage 1 teachers argue that they are unhappy at the stress experienced by seven-year olds. But others tell me that it is really a matter of how teachers, and headteachers in particular, feel. If the head communicates his/her stress to the teachers, then they are likely to pass this tension on to the children. But there is no reason why it has to be like this. Nor am I persuaded by arguments that the tests do not do justice to those aspects of the Orders that they set out to test. No test can assess every curricular objective effectively, but it is perfectly feasible to construct tests which do assess key objectives in English, mathematics and science in a valid and reliable way. OFSTED has written recently about the rigour and imagination of the mathematics tests at Key Stage 3. The General Secretary of the National Association for the Teaching of English has spoken positively of the way the English tests have been developed and of how they now constitute a valid measure of pupil achievement. The National Curriculum tests may not be perfect, but they cannot be dismissed as educationally unsound.

Workload

The issue of the additional workload required by National Curriculum assessment continues to be a major factor in the dispute over the tests. As a point of fact, SCAA has reduced the amount of marking and administration time which the tests involve by well over 50 per cent from 1993 to 1994. For a class of 30 children, it would have taken 24 hours for a Key Stage 1 teacher to mark the English and mathematics papers, 47 hours for a Key Stage 2 teacher to mark the English, mathematics and science tests and, at Key Stage 3, up to 10 hours to mark each of the English, mathematics, and science tests. In 1995, we have seen the introduction of external marking at Key Stages 2 and 3 (with supply cover at Key Stage 1). This has largely removed the problem of workload. The main argument against external marking appears to be the loss of diagnostic information about a pupil's strengths and weaknesses. This has been dealt with by returning the scripts.

A further argument against external marking has been that it will devalue teacher assessment, but it is difficult to see why this need be the case. Some commentators (such as the NAHT) link the proposal to end the auditing of teacher assessment to this assertion. In fact, the validity of this decision depends upon a judgement about the benefits which these exercises bestow and the amount of teacher time taken up by them. On the former, most teachers I have talked to believe that audit/moderation meetings have been an important form of professional development. If this is so, then there is no reason why schools cannot use their own in-service resources to ensure, by some means, that this form of professional development continues. There is less agreement about whether the significant time involved is justified in terms of the audit function. The SCAA's consultation on different approaches to this question at Key Stage 3 certainly suggests that schools would favour a minimalist approach to the audit. This might involve, say, the publication of a non-statutory statement of good assessment practice, but would not require schools to attend moderation meetings. Be that as it may, it is hard to see why the introduction of external marking should necessarily devalue teacher assessment: there are a number of ways in which standards of teacher assessment can be secured without the current moderation arrangements and without suggesting that the status of teacher assessment is in some way inferior.

Performance tables

My conclusion is that we have an overall approach to assessment which draws upon the strengths of both tests and teacher assessment. We have tests which are educationally sound. A solution to the workload question is also in sight. The issue of performance tables remains more contentious: it is clear that many teachers continue to be concerned about the publication of data drawn from the National Curriculum tests. Their concern is, basically, that there is no way of making allowance for the fact that schools serving different communities are not competing one with another on a level playing field. The objection is to the genuineness of the comparisons, rather than to the principle of opening up relative performance to public scrutiny.

In my view, the absolute objection is hard to sustain. I accept that schools are not concerned solely with the academic achievement of their pupils. Other objectives concerning, for example, moral or spiritual development, are less easy to quantify, but still enormously important. But academic teaching, on anyone's definition of the purposes of education, must be a school's core business. We know that schools serving similar communities can achieve markedly different academic results. Should not parents know how well a school is teaching its pupils before they make a choice for their child? And should not those in local and central government know how well or how badly the schools for which they are responsible are doing? Only when that information is known can appropriate action be taken and support provided. To those who reject arguments based on parental choice on the grounds that, in reality, choice is limited to the fortunate few, I can only reply that this is no reason why test data should not be published. It merely shows how important it is that standards of education in average and mediocre schools are raised so that the pressure on the successful schools is eased and the extent of choice widened. Nor is it inevitable, as some fear, that a market-driven economy will destroy all collaboration between schools. As a point of historical fact, there never was a golden age of co-operation. Schools have always, naturally and inevitably, put the interests of their own pupils first. It would be wrong for them to do otherwise. But this does not mean that now or in the future the world of education must be characterized by cut-throat hostility. In my experience, schools and colleges in many areas are co-operating better across the phases than has been the case in the past. I refer here both to secondary schools working with their feeder primaries, and to secondary schools and colleges planning a coherent 14–19 curriculum. Within the phases themselves, where competition would (and should) be sharpest, we have impressive examples of headteachers working out codes of practice which define fair play. As schools use the time created by the Dearing Review to specialize in particular aspects of the curriculum, concepts of competition will become more sophisticated: there will be a gradual shift from a comparison of a common provision to choices between the kind of curriculum emphases on offer. But the most telling argument for the publication of test data is that it can act as a powerful motivator. Headteachers or governors who study the tables and realize that nearby schools serving similar communities are achieving better results will inevitably be driven to ask challenging questions about what is going wrong in their own schools. Competition can be a strong catalyst to new thinking and greater effort.

For these reasons, I support the drive to render school performance more open and the system more accountable. It may well be that we can develop a value-added approach to the publication of data. There are dangers here (for example, of excessive statistical complexity or of trying to utilize complex socio-economical inputs), but, if these dangers can be overcome, then the result would help to encourage more teachers to see the National Curriculum tests as a positive and useful element within the assessment framework and to remove resistance within the profession to the performance tables.

Conclusion

The National Curriculum and its assessment arrangements lie at the heart of the drive to raise standards of educational achievement. But the words on the page of the National Curriculum Orders will in themselves achieve nothing. Everything depends upon how teachers translate these words into effective classroom practice. This truism is nonetheless a useful reminder to advisers, LEA officers, civil servants and politicians of how remote they are from the real point of influence.

If everything depends on teachers and schools, what are the implications? Do we have the policies and initiatives in place to support the profession in their task of translating the National Curriculum into classroom reality? The key priorities as I see them are as follows: first, irrespective of the relative responsibilities of schools and Institutes of Higher Education, the reform of initial teacher training must be taken forward so that all teachers are equipped with both the subject knowledge which the National Curriculum requires and the pedagogic skills which are essential to effective classroom practice. Second, in-service resources must continue to be targeted on those aspects of the teaching of the National Curriculum and its assessment that are proving problematic. This means a fundamental re-appraisal of the capacity of LEAs, post-LMS and GMS, to support schools, and a review of the strategies open to us if we are to fill gaps where support is not being provided. Third, given the key responsibility of the headteacher for curriculum leadership and resource management, we need far better training for headship than yet exists. Fourth, since all organizations benefit from a periodic external review, it is in everyone's interests that the work of OFSTED is carried through successfully.

There is nothing new on this agenda. This in itself is important, for the last thing the education service now needs is further radical policy change. The basic principles which underpinned the 1988 and 1992 Education Acts (the definition of the national specification as to what should be taught; the devolution of maximum possible responsibility for the achievement of this specification to the individual school; the development of systems of accountability) point the right way forward. The task now – for all of us who work within education – is to ensure that the reforms of the last six years are actually made to work.

4

The National Curriculum and the Policy Process

Sheila Dainton

Introduction

Policy analysis is a complex business. It can also be highly subjective. Wherever we stand to survey the political landscape, we start from a relativist position, informed by a host of antecedents and personal pre-dilections which have influenced and dictated individual perceptions of the 'reality' of a situation. It is rarely possible to agree on one version of events: the most that can be achieved is a credible interpretation. It is no easier to capture policy-making and policy-implementing in a series of snapshots or cameos than it is to photograph the ethos of a school. The best we can do is to gather together points of view from as many angles – and as many quarters – as possible, try to build a picture of the whole, and then attempt to make some sense of it.

In writing this chapter, my intention is threefold: to set down what the National Curriculum was, what it is, and what it might become; to offer a credible interpretation of events, contextualized in my own subjectivity, from the viewpoint of a trade-union official, employed by what is gener-ally regarded as a moderate teacher union; and to offer a perspective on the role of teachers' unions in influencing the National Curriculum.

This account is written from an office only a stone's throw away from the Houses of Parliament, where education policy is enshrined in statute, and just around the corner from Sanctuary Buildings, workplace for thousands of Department for Education and Employment (DFEE) civil servants. Among them are officials who played a critical role in deter-mining the shape of the National Curriculum and in pushing through its implementation. The rapid turnover in education ministers since 1988 has given senior civil servants all the more scope to influence the political agenda and, if Rita Webb (1994) is correct, to act as the guardians of education regulations and legislation. The most frustrating aspect of the current situation is the dearth of clear evidence about the private agendas of civil servants (for while they might be 'neutered', they are surely far from neutral) and their motives in influencing education policy. For the time being, at least, their side of the story remains untold.

Policy is a process as well as a product. As Ham and Hill (1984) point out, policy is frequently made during what is conventionally described as the implementation stage of the policy process – and this has certainly been the case with the National Curriculum. The process is rarely logical and entirely rational, nor does it always progress in neat, incremental steps. In describing the relationship between rationality and decision-making, it is not always easy to distinguish between what the theorists call 'bounded rationality' or 'incrementalism' and what, in practice, seems more like wilful bloody-mindedness, or a zealous enthusiasm to bolt one piece of legislation on to the next, regardless of coherence or what Her Majesty's Inspectors might call fitness for purpose. So far as recent education reforms are concerned, it is difficult to discern any clear relationship between rationality and decision-making in the policy process. Policies were formulated without first establishing a clear set of principles and an explicit value base, and they were not based on extensive research and clear analysis. As Sayer (1993) points out, claims were made that markets, choice and diversity are all about raising standards. There is, however, no substantive evidence that one automatically follows the other. Although it was claimed that the National Curriculum, of itself, would raise standards, there was no debate about what was meant by standards, or whose standards were to be adopted.

As time moves on, teachers should get better at teaching the National Curriculum, and pupils should get better at learning it, and being tested on it. Unless something goes dreadfully amiss, standards in teaching and learning the National Curriculum will improve. We cannot, however, deduce from this the simplistic and untested assumption that standards in, for example, the quality of intellectual thought, or in the application of logic, will necessarily get better, nor – as is often implied – that the country's economic performance will show a marked improvement. The relationship between cause and effect needs to be rooted in evidence, not rhetoric.

We are at the beginning of an analysis of the consequences of educational reforms. As far as the policy process and the National Curriculum are concerned, there are many with stories to tell who are beginning to offer credible interpretations. These include a former Secretary of State for Education (Baker, 1993); the former Chairman and Chief Executive of the National Curriculum Council (NCC) (Graham and Tytler, 1993); the former holder of the post of Her Majesty's Chief Inspector (Bolton, 1994a); former members of the government-appointed working groups set up to design the National Curriculum and its tests (for example, Black, 1992; Marenbon, 1993); and the accounts of teachers whose professional lives were considerably affected by the sheer volume of work arising from rapid implementation of the National Curriculum Orders (Campbell *et al.*, 1991; Webb, 1993). Everyone has a story to tell.

What is the National Curriculum?

Events leading to the inclusion in the 1988 Education Reform Act (ERA) of Sections on the National Curriculum have been well documented (see, for example, Aldrich, 1988; Maclure, 1988; Chitty, 1993; Pollard *et al.*, 1994, and many others). All accounts agree on one central issue: moves towards more centralized control over the structure and delivery of the school curriculum were the belated product of Prime Minister James Callaghan's seminal speech delivered at Ruskin College, Oxford, on 18 October 1976.

As Chitty (1993) points out, it is tempting – but wrong – to locate the origins of the Conservative government's 1988 National Curriculum in Callaghan's speech. Indeed, as late as March 1985 the government issued a White Paper (DES, 1985) which confirmed that: 'It would not in the view of the Government be right for the Secretaries of State's policy for the range and pattern of the 5–16 curriculum to amount to the determination of national syllabuses for that period.' Chitty goes on to show that it was relatively late in the day that the then Secretary of State for Education, Kenneth Baker, supported by civil servants from the Department for Education and Science (DES), came up with a National Curriculum framework listing ten foundation subjects to be taken by all pupils during their compulsory education.

The legislative intention on the curriculum is set down in the first four Sections of the ERA. The first Section explains in broad terms the requirements which the curriculum for any maintained school should satisfy. The curriculum should be balanced and broadly based and should:

(a) promote the spiritual, moral, cultural, mental and physical development of pupils at the school and of society; and

(b) prepare such pupils for the opportunities, responsibilities and experiences of adult life.

Just what was meant by 'the spiritual, moral, cultural, mental and physical', and how the curriculum of a school should promote these (particularly the first three) has never been entirely clear. But it was not the intention, as later stated by the SCAA (1994a), that religious education should, *inter alia*, promote the physical development of pupils. The phrase 'and of society' is included almost as a throwaway line. There was little discussion about how the school curriculum should be orientated to the needs of adult life, nor was there agreement about the typical predicaments of adult life.

Section 2 of the Act explains that the National Curriculum is part of the 'basic' curriculum – essentially, the National Curriculum subjects plus religious education. It also states that the National Curriculum should specify the 'arrangements for assessing pupils at or near the end of each key stage'. The Act did not create SATs. There is nothing in primary legislation about key stage tests, standard assessment tasks, teacher assessment or tick boxes. ERA simply states that assessment should ascertain what pupils have achieved in relation to attainment targets for each key stage. Section 3 sets down the subject areas for the foundation subjects and defines the four key stages, and Section 4 requires the Secretary of State to establish a complete National Curriculum 'as soon as is reasonably practicable' and to revise that curriculum 'whenever he considers it necessary or expedient to do so'.

The original National Curriculum comprised:

(a) foundation subjects – including three core subjects and seven other foundation subjects;

(b) attainment targets (later specified up to 10 levels of attainment) covering the ages 5–16, setting objectives for learning;

(c) programmes of study specifying essential teaching within each subject area;

(d) assessment arrangements (later related to 10 levels of attainment).

The statutory Orders for attainment targets, programmes of study and assessment arrangements relate requirements to the four key stages, which cover approximately the two infant years (Key Stage 1), the four junior years (Key Stage 2), the first three years of secondary schooling (Key Stage 3) and the final two years of compulsory schooling (Key Stage 4). These key stages are the same whatever the local school organization and irrespective of local school transfer ages.

The National Curriculum and the school day

It was never envisaged that the National Curriculum would take up all the taught time. Answering a question during the passage of the Education Reform Bill which preceded the Act, Angela Rumbold (1987), Minister for State at the DES, stated that the National Curriculum was intended to be contained within about 70 per cent of the school curriculum time. Equally, the government could not prescribe how much time should be devoted to individual subjects (see Section 4(3)(a) of the ERA), but some initial guidance was clearly necessary.

The government's consultative document on the National Curriculum (DES, 1987) stated that, at primary level, the 'majority of curriculum time' should be devoted to the three core subjects of science, mathematics and English. An illustrative table included in the consultative document allocates between 75 and 85 per cent of curriculum time to the

foundation subjects in the secondary phase. The working groups established to produce the subject Orders were given 'notional' guidance
about the time assumed to be available for each foundation subject and
religious education (RE) which left between 5 and 10 per cent of time
for 'other' learning. According to DES Circular 5/89 (DES, 1989a), from
the 1989 autumn term all the foundation subjects and RE were expected
to have 'reasonable time' devoted to them, but percentages were not
specified.

By the end of 1991 the NCC publicly recognized that there were a
number of 'pressing issues' at primary level, including problems of
manageability, complexity and over-prescription. These issues are high-
lighted in the Council's first (and last) Corporate Plan (NCC, 1991).
However, it came as something of a surprise when, two years later, at
a time when curriculum overload at the primary level had been publicly
acknowledged by the NCC, David Pascall (1993), the Council's Chairman, announced to an audience of primary teachers in Oxford that he
had 'come to the view' that the National Curriculum should occupy no
more than 70 per cent of school time. He did not seem to appreciate
that the government had never intended it to be otherwise.

Setting up the National Curriculum

Several months before the ERA was placed on the statute books,
arrangements were set in train to ensure that the National Curriculum
was up and running as quickly as possible. The seeds of future problems
were sown when, in May 1988, two new shadow bodies were set up – the
NCC in York and the School Examination and Assessment Council
(SEAC) in London – with members appointed directly by the Secretary
of State; they were both properly established in August 1988. It did not
take long before the Councils, which became as far apart philosophically
as they were geographically, became the focus of distracting and debil-
itating power struggles. Before the NCC and the SEAC were established
the working groups set up to create the National Curriculum for mathematics, science and English (also appointed directly by the Secretary
of State) worked against the clock between the autumn of 1987 and
summer 1988 to meet tight deadlines. As Duncan Graham (Graham and
Tytler, 1993), Chairman and Chief Executive of the NCC from its foundation in 1988 until July 1991, reminds us, the working groups' remit
was that they would be required within a matter of only a few months
to determine what society would expect a child to know in the three core
subjects at the ages of 7, 11, 14 and 16 and would form the basis of what
was to be taught in 24,000 state schools in England and Wales. Between
September 1987 and March 1988 a Task Group on Assessment and
Testing (TGAT) devised a system combining teachers' own formative

assessments with standard assessment tasks (SATs), charting pupils' progress on a 10-level scale. At the time, the TGAT proposals were widely welcomed by the teaching profession: they were not the narrowly focused pencil-and-paper tests that many had feared.

To demonstrate the pace and, more importantly, the caution at which work was being undertaken, it is worth noting the contents of a letter from Professor Paul Black, Chairman of TGAT, to Kenneth Baker (then Secretary of State for Education), written on Christmas Eve, 1987 (DES, 1988a). The letter, which is a preface to the main report of the Task Group, states:

> Because of the short time available we have not been able to give adequate attention to one part of our remit: we are not yet in a position to make recommendations about the various services and arrangements required to support the system that we propose. We discuss some of the issues involved in the enclosed report, but we would like to give more considered advice about these in about two months time.

TGAT submitted three supplementary reports to the Secretary of State (DES, 1988b), the third of which, 'A System of Support', proposes a comprehensive plan of support requirements for an assessment and testing, considered in the context of the wider development of the National Curriculum. However, the report received scant attention from ministers and was quickly buried. As Peter Watkins (1993), former Deputy Chief Executive of the NCC pointed out, the National Curriculum had no architect, only builders. Taking the analogy further, it was not deemed necessary for the builders to have access to any quantity surveyors. Given the enormity of the task in hand, this is, with hindsight, quite alarming.

The speed of implementation

In his account of the intrigue and pressure that marked the introduction of the National Curriculum, Graham (Graham and Tytler, 1993) points to the massive shift in the way in which curriculum developments at a national level were to happen. In the past, committees set up by the DES to consider a specific subject or area of education would frequently sit for two years or more, perhaps deciding in the end that no changes in the *status quo* were required. Under the NCC things changed overnight and Kenneth Baker was having none of that. Graham states that: 'The government was going to insist that the job was done and that for the most part it was done the government's way.' However, Graham had accepted the post of Chairman and Chief Executive on the basis of rapid implementation of the National Curriculum and made no apology for it at the time.

The speed with which the National Curriculum was put together and implemented was a recipe for disaster. Since 1987, and under five successive Secretaries of State, a powerful sense of urgency and a compelling drive to push things forward regardless of problems and near-disasters have been chilling features of the political pressure to which education is now subject. The process envisaged was that of a machine-driven production line, punctuated only with rushed consultations with near-impossible deadlines. It seemed that all that was necessary to reform the curriculum was that it should be written, packaged, posted and, finally, 'delivered' by teachers in schools. It was a example of what Popper (1945) calls 'utopian engineering' which went disastrously wrong. Moreover, for those who could see it (and this includes some members of the original science, mathematics and English working parties), the unmanageability of the whole curriculum was predictable from the serial mode of its invention. Each of the government-appointed subject working groups was required to make recommendations for the programmes of study in one subject in isolation from other groups, with nobody, not even, apparently, the NCC, according to Duncan Graham, being allowed to accept formal responsibility for monitoring the overall demands. It could, however, be argued that Duncan Graham's unwillingness or his inability to insist upon that formal responsibility – without which he could not begin to do his job properly – is a measure of his failure.

It is difficult, and perhaps unhelpful, to attempt to apportion blame for the woefully inadequate and often cack-handed way in which the original National Curriculum was 'designed'. The real locus of power in the early days of National Curriculum implementation is difficult to pin down and the buck-passing has still not stopped, with blame being passed from one civil servant or former minister to the next. At the end of the day it was teachers who were on the receiving end of mismanagement of the highest order. As Campbell and Neill (1994a) conclude: 'The curriculum invented and implemented serially had become, for those obliged to implement it, a serial killer.'

Why a 10-subject curriculum?

The absence of a carefully reasoned foundation to the proposals was a fundamental cause for concern which was never the subject of genuine public debate. What was then the Assistant Masters' and Mistresses' Association (AMMA, 1987) said in response to the original consultation on the National Curriculum proposals: 'To suggest that a national curriculum rooted in the discrete academic disciplines historically studied by grammar school pupils will, by the mere addition of technology, raise the educational standards of all the country's children is simplistic and naive.'

Lord Joseph, the former Education Secretary, was later to lead a robust revolt against the National Curriculum in the House of Lords but was rewarded with a crushing defeat. During the debate on the Education Reform Bill he lined up behind an Opposition amendment to free the curriculum from its compulsory 'strait-jacket' by making it something schools had to 'have regard to' but could depart from. He argued that the proposed curriculum would particularly damage non-academic children, and added that it conflicted sharply with the government's own philosophy that it should simply set the framework and leave people to follow their own purposes within it, an argument later pursued by John Marenbon (1993), an active member of the right-wing Centre for Policy Studies (CPS) and one-time member of the Secretary of State's English working group. Lord Joseph rightly predicted that the proposals before Parliament would 'impose on those who work with children a quite intolerable burden' (quoted in the *Telegraph*, 4 May 1988). But 218 Lords voted against the amendment and 144 in favour – making a government majority of 74 (reported in *The Times Educational Supplement*, 6 May 1988).

Getting the show on the road

Early warnings from teachers, the so-called educational establishment, and many others, catalogued by Haviland (1988), were almost wilfully ignored. The environment in which the National Curriculum was being developed became increasingly anti-intellectual, with talk of 'simple language' and 'teacher-friendly' publications. The implication was that teachers were to be spoon-fed – rather than intellectually stimulated and challenged – by the National Curriculum. The atmosphere was one of 'we must get this show on the road at all costs'. An impressive carpet bearing the NCC's monogram appeared at Albion Wharf, the Council's York headquarters, and the NCC mounted a series of roadshows, complete with the paraphernalia of a Sunday School outing, including balloons, NCC T-shirts and monogrammed plastic carrier bags. At the same time, lessons which could – indeed should – have been drawn from the burgeoning literature on the management of change were completely disregarded and pile upon pile of what Secretary of State John MacGregor (1990) was later to call 'co-ordinated bumf' landed on staffroom tables. As a teachers' union colleague commented at an early meeting with the NCC: 'This is no way to run a railway.'

Sensibly planned, the National Curriculum had the potential to create a sense of public ownership of education, raising the status of teaching and schooling, and providing sound criteria against which issues of accountability, effectiveness and improvement could be judged. That was not to be so. Right from the start the National Curriculum was dogged by a persistent, blind and – perhaps worst of all – an extraordinarily arrogant belief on the part of civil servants and ministers of state that they knew more about the nuts and bolts of curriculum development, and about the management of change in schools, than teachers, local education authorities, academics and researchers, all of whom (particularly the latter two) soon came to be regarded with a degree of hostility, if not downright contempt. Worst of all, it would appear that no one with the positional power to do so had the confidence to tell ministers they were wrong, or the guts to resign in protest. The atmosphere in which the National Curriculum was introduced into schools was heavy-handed and punitive, with finger-wagging civil servants insisting that 'no-one liked change but things would settle down'. Teachers were expected to knuckle under and tackle the impossible. What, with hindsight, is surprising is just how many of them did precisely that – and with a vengeance.

The whole curriculum

The original plan was that there should be nine foundation subjects taught across Key Stages 1 and 2, with a modern foreign language added at Key Stages 3 and 4 and with assessment at the end of each key stage. But that was not all. In the early days of implementation, the NCC and the DES went to great lengths to acknowledge the original legislative intention and to set the National Curriculum in the context of the whole school curriculum.

The DES publication *From Policy to Practice* (DES, 1989b) stresses that the foundation subjects are 'certainly not' a complete curriculum. It goes on to say: 'They are not sufficient to ensure a curriculum which meets the purposes and covers the elements identified by HMI and others' and to spell out the need for key cross-curricular competencies (literacy, numeracy and IT skills), themes such as economic awareness, political and international understanding and environmental education, and coverage across the curriculum of gender and multi-cultural issues.

From Policy to Practice was followed by the NCC booklet *Curriculum Guidance 3: The Whole Curriculum* (NCC, 1990) which highlights the 'pressing' need for the defining of a whole curriculum. It states that schools should seek to identify the considerable overlaps which 'inevitably' exist both in content and skills in the National Curriculum foundation subjects (surely, first and foremost, a job for the NCC, not for schools) and goes on to suggest that, in due course, schools are likely to 'throw all the attainment targets in a heap on the floor and reassemble them in a way which provides for them the very basis of a whole curriculum' – something which most primary teachers found necessary anyway. There was much said and written about cross-curricular elements, dimensions, skills and themes, and schools were encouraged to use the NCC's guidance to identify cross-curricular provision, links between subjects, and to develop, review and evaluate a school policy for the whole curriculum.

The demise of the whole curriculum

Given its importance only seven years ago, it is somewhat alarming that the whole curriculum is barely mentioned in the revised 'new' National Curriculum documents which have recently become the subject of consultation (SCAA, 1994b). Cross-curricular dimensions and skills have all but disappeared from official publications, and cross-curricular themes, which in earlier days featured strongly in successive policy statements, have been pushed to the margins – even though many schools spent valuable time and energy trying to implement them in accordance with the NCC's earlier advice. Towards the end of its life, and after two years of constant badgering from the teachers' associations, the NCC prepared an eight-page document 'The National Curriculum: An Overview of the Cross-Curricular Themes' (NCC, 1992). Although it reached proof stage in November 1992, the document was never published. This suggests one of three things: the NCC's earlier work on cross-curricular skills, themes and dimensions was largely cosmetic and a sop to teachers; the NCC was genuinely concerned about the way it had overloaded the curriculum; or that the whole philosophy of the Council, which, particularly since the appointment of David Pascall as Chairman, became increasingly politically rather than educationally dominated, had a distinct preference for a no-nonsense, straight down the line, subject-by-subject curriculum.

The cross-curricular themes, dimensions and skills threatened to overwhelm an already overweight curriculum. Ministers were against them (rumour has it that former Education Minister Emily Blatch went purple every time she heard the term) and wanted to press on with the subjects alone. The themes and dimensions have been quietly buried, while the cross-curricular skills are now caught up in the debate about General National Vocational Qualifications (GNVQ) and vocational routes.

From the end of 1992 the whole curriculum became someone else's problem, but no one said whose. It was left for schools to hold on to, and build upon, the original legislative intention. It is sometimes forgotten that the provision by schools of a balanced and broadly based whole curriculum is a statutory requirement, not just an ideal to aim for.

Assessment and testing

In terms of assessment, the TGAT model has been slowly but surely corroded: 'death by a thousand cuts', as Professor Paul Black (1992) Chairman of the Task Group has described it. The original idea, clearly articulated in the TGAT report, was that assessment should be the 'servant' not the 'master' of the curriculum. It should be an integral part of the educational process, continually providing both 'feedback' and 'feedforward' (DES, 1988a). The main purpose of assessment, according to the TGAT report, was 'formative' – to help teachers identify children's achievements and plan the next steps in learning. However, the emphasis on the summative end of key stage tests is subverting the formative element of assessment. Teacher assessment – seen by many teachers as the key tool for raising standards in education – has been overshadowed by the emphasis upon, and the controversy surrounding, the statutory tests.

The national debate about assessment and testing, such as it was, moved quickly – and blindly – away from a discussion genuinely rooted in exploring the key purposes of any national system of assessment and in looking at what is already known about the relationship between learning and assessment. Questions about the perceived inherent tensions in a system designed to be both formative and summative have never been properly addressed. The teachers' unions have necessarily become critically involved in the 'simplification' debate, triggered ostensibly by concerns about workloads arising from the National Curriculum and its assessment, but in reality by a very different set of concerns about the Key Stage 3 English curriculum. The government has addressed the workload issue with a pragmatic, quick-fix solution, with a package that includes committing over £30 million to the appointment of external markers for Key Stage 2 and 3 tests and providing additional funding for supply cover at Key Stage 1. With the introduction of external markers announced in September 1994, the withdrawal of a government grant specifically earmarked to support teachers' own assessments, and with the government's continued commitment to league tables at 11, there is a serious danger that what is left on the assessment front will be little short of narrowly focused external tests with progression and differentiation no longer taken seriously. This is the fearful prospect which TGAT foresaw but strove to avoid. What is politically available has taken precedence over what many teachers believe to be educationally desirable. The real debate on testing and assessment is still in its infancy.

Religious education

One subject which, perhaps surprisingly, has benefited from the National Curriculum is RE. Although not a foundation subject, far more clauses of the ERA are devoted to RE and collective worship (consistently, but unhelpfully, grouped together) than to the rest of the National Curriculum. By all accounts Duncan Graham was not a great RE enthusiast, neither was Chris Woodhead in his earlier role as the second

Chief Executive of NCC. However, David Pascall, a committed Christian and Chairman of the NCC from 1991–3, was determined to put RE high on the agenda. Speaking from a text riddled with religious imagery, Pascall (1992) talks of the original 'vision' of the ERA, about 'rocks upon which we can build for the future'. For Pascall, Section 1 of the ERA, with its emphasis on pupils' spiritual, moral, cultural, mental and physical development, is the vision 'enshrined' in legislation. From 1992, the emphasis shifted away from the whole curriculum and cross-curricular themes and towards the ten foundation subjects, RE, and the moral and the spiritual.

At about the same time an insistence on the importance of moral and religious education was running through the White Paper *Choice and Diversity* (DFE, 1992). By March 1993 the NCC had issued schools with a discussion paper on spiritual and moral development (NCC, 1993). The ten-page paper said little that was new. It failed to acknowledge that teachers – and others – had given very serious thought to these issues for many, many years. Several teachers were so bemused that they telephoned the *Guardian* (reported in the *Guardian*, 2 April 1993) to ask whether the paper's report on the (then leaked) document was an April Fool joke. By this time spirituality and morality had become firmly yoked together and the importance of RE to moral development was being re-asserted. Underlying the political rhetoric about RE over the last few years has been the suggestion that an essential reason for reinforcing the teaching of religion – and particularly Christianity – is to improve moral and social standards. It is sometimes forgotten that children have a right in law to be educated in religion, just as they have a right to be educated in, say, mathematics or science. Education in religion should be a serious, open and balanced study of the subject. However, the child's right to be 'religiously educated' has not always been central to the debate about RE which, increasingly, has been strongly influenced by a small but powerful lobby group, members of which were both politically and theologically to the far right of the political spectrum. Too often, valuable debating time has been devoted to a fruitless controversy about the percentage of time accorded to Christianity.

As a result of work initiated by the NCC, the School Curriculum and Assessment Authority (SCAA) produced two model syllabuses for RE which were published in July 1994. By and large, the models have been well received by the RE community. However, Hargreaves (1994) argues that a more fundamental question has yet to be addressed: is it necessary for the education system to articulate a common core of values shared across communities in a pluralistic society, and if so, how is this best achieved in schools? Increasingly, RE and the clutter of the National Curriculum Orders is proving a distraction from, rather than an answer to, this question.

Continuity and progression?

The Conservative Party has been in power since May 1979. Putting to one side the fact that some Conservatives see the change over from Thatcher to Major in November 1990 as a change of government, this is the longest any political party has been in power since 1830; when Grey replaced Wellington, ending twenty-three years of Tory rule. But, if enhanced continuity and progression were intended to be a hallmark of the National Curriculum, they have certainly not characterized those bodies responsible to government for translating the broad brush of national legislation into a workable reality in schools. There appears to be barely a handful of key individuals at a national level in the policy-making and policy-implementing process with a first-hand sense of history dating back to the early days of the National Curriculum when the Education Reform Bill (GERBIL, as it was then known) was being debated in Parliament.

In his fascinating analysis of what was then perceived to be the role of the political head of the education service, Kogan (1971) makes the obvious but important point that to work out and work through a new pattern of educational development requires time and expertise. Kogan quotes Anthony Crosland, Secretary of State for Education and Science between January 1965 and August 1967, on the time-scale of politics and policy formation. Crosland says: 'I reckon it takes you six months to get your head properly above water, a year to get the general drift of most of the field, and two years really to master the whole of a Department.' On the basis of this analysis, since the introduction of the National Curriculum in 1988 only two of the recent secretaries of state for education has had an opportunity to 'master' the Department for which he (or later, she) was ultimately responsible. John Patten held the job for just over two years. However, the extent to which he genuinely got a grip on education policy and 'mastered' the whole of the DES (and, later, the DFE) remains very much open to question. Of the five secretaries of state for education who have been in post since the National Curriculum was introduced in 1988; only two have held office for more than two years:

Kenneth Baker	July 1986–July 1989
John MacGregor	July 1989–November 1990
Kenneth Clarke	November 1990–April 1992
John Patten	April 1992–July 1994
Gillian Shephard	July 1994–

During the same period there have been four permanent secretaries at the DES/DFE:

Sir David Hancock   May 1983–June 1989
Sir John Caines   July 1989–January 1993
Sir Geoffrey Holland   January 1993–January 1994
Sir Timothy Lankester   February 1994–

In their relatively short lives (which, including the two 'shadow' Councils, span from May 1988 to September 1993) the NCC and SEAC had, between them, four chief executives, one acting chief executive and six chairmen:

NCC
Duncan Graham	Chairman and Chief Executive, May 1988–July 1991
Chris Woodhead	Chief Executive, July 1991–September 1993
David Pascall	Chairman, July 1991–April 1993
Sir Ron Dearing	Chairman, April 1993–September 1993

SEAC
Philip Halsey	Chairman and Chief Executive, May 1988–July 1991
Richard Dorrance	Acting Chief Executive, July 1991–December 1991
Hilary Nicolle	Chief Executive, January 1992–September 1993
Lord Griffiths of Fforestfach	Chairman, July 1991–April 1993
Sir Ron Dearing	Chairman, April 1993–September 1993

SCAA's Chief Executive, Chris Woodhead, took on the job of Her Majesty's Chief Inspector (HMCI) from 1 October 1994 after barely a year in post. His predecessor at the Office for Standards in Education (OFSTED), the former HMCI Professor Stewart Sutherland, left the job after only two years.

At the DES – as in all Whitehall departments – it was *de rigueur* for officials to be moved on from one job to the next, seemingly in a deliberate attempt to discourage any individual from getting to grips with, and taking an ideological line on, an educational issue. The culture of constant re-shuffling is no different at the DFE which, having been created in July 1992, has already undergone a major structural reorganization, largely as the result of the formation of the SCAA. A review of the role of the DFE, commissioned by the Department and conducted by Coopers and Lybrand, has subsequently been undertaken (DFE, 1993) and in the summer of 1995 the DFE was merged with the Department of Employment and another structural reorganization began.

The irony, of course, is that this succession of ministers and civil servants has had statutory responsibility to design and implement a curriculum based on a philosophy of continuity and progression. Constant chopping and changing at national level, with successive ministers interfering with the detail of the curriculum, makes nonsense of the concept at the very heart of recent education legislation. It also fails to address one of the most serious flaws in the policy-making and policy-implementing process: the proclivity of those with both power and *de jure* responsibility to move on before they face the consequences of their own decisions and actions. Little wonder, then, that many teachers, having approached the National Curriculum with cautious optimism, now regard the decision-makers with increasing cynicism. Any school managed with the ineptitude shown by those responsible for the education service at a national level would be branded as 'failing' and quickly brought to heel – or closed down – by government inspectors.

ERA: the definitive Act?

At the time of its passage through Parliament, the ERA was heralded as the definitive piece of post-Butler legislation which would last until the end of the twentieth century. But this was not to be so. Only three years later the School Teachers' Pay and Conditions Act 1991 created the School Teachers' Review Body (STRB) and put an end to collective bargaining in the schools' sector. The following year the Further and Higher Education Act 1992 placed further and higher education in the hands of two new quangos – the Further Education Funding Council (FEFC) and the Higher Education Funding Council (HEFC) – and the Education (Schools) Act 1992 all but killed off Her Majesty's Inspectorate and created OFSTED.

The Funding Agency for Schools (FAS) was created under the 1993 Education Act, which was heralded in Secretary of State John Patten's White Paper (DFE, 1992) as legislation that would bring us into the next century. Patten promised it would be 'the last piece of the jig-saw', a phrase used two years later by Secretary of State Gillian Shephard when Key Stage 2 statutory tests were introduced. The Act included sections on school admissions, the procedure for acquisition of grant-maintained status, the provision of further education in grant-maintained schools, and special educational needs. The final part of the Act comprises a lengthy miscellaneous section covering everything from nursery education in grant-maintained schools to the replacement of the NCC and SEAC by the SCAA. Finally, the 1994 Education Act removed the funding of initial teacher training in England from the HEFC for England and established in its place a Teacher Training Agency which was also responsible for providing information and advice on teaching as a career, and accreditation.

The picture on the whole jigsaw still remains unclear. As former Chief HMI Eric Bolton (1994b) has commented: 'No-one seems to have any idea what our education service might look like, or is intended to be, say by the year 2010.' In particular, the interrelationship and the balance of power between at least four of the quangos set up by central Government (SCAA, the National Council for Vocational Qualifications (NCVQ), FAS and, importantly, the STRB) seems uncertain, as do the institutional and structural relationships between these quangos, OFSTED, the DFEE and, of course, local education authorities. The situation is ripe for confusion, conflict, power struggles and in-fighting. The increasing spread of power and responsibility away from local education authorities and towards government-appointed quangos, all closely shadowed by the DFEE, makes it all the more likely that the right hand will not know what the left is doing. This is not good for coherent policy development and sensibly planned policy-implementation, and it is certainly not helpful for teachers and schools.

Looking back, it seems that the absence of a coherent education policy within the Conservative Party, or within the DES/DFEE, allowed a succession of education ministers to reach for the statute book every time they panicked or had a new idea – and before they had worked out the detail of what they wanted. The situation is one of chronic unpredictability and uncertainty. It is as if policy-making in education has become some kind of ball game played on a muddy field with a lot of people pushing and shoving. Everyone has forgotten that the name of the game is to score goals.

Conversion on the road to Cardiff?

On the morning of 7 April 1993, Secretary of State John Patten addressed the Association of Teachers and Lecturers (ATL) Assembly – the Association's supreme policy-making body – at St David's Hall in Cardiff (ATL, 1993). The Minister received a polite but muted welcome. Only five days earlier, the High Court had declared that the industrial action on grounds of excessive workloads being taken by the National Association of Schoolmasters and Union of Women Teachers (NASUWT) was lawful. The ATL's Assembly was on the verge of deciding whether to ballot the Association's members on limiting workload to an acceptable level. Members agreed to postpone their decision until after John Patten had spoken. The Minister promised that it would be: 'a longish speech, with no peroration, but it will contain a very important and detailed announcement'. He spoke of the appointment of a serving classroom teacher to SCAA, to which Assembly responded 'only one!', and went on to say that he was writing that day to Sir Ron Dearing (a couple of weeks in advance of Dearing's appointment as joint Chairman of NCC and SEAC) 'to outline areas I wish him to concentrate upon in helping the Government to meet their objective of having a National Curriculum and an associated testing regime that are as slim and as effective as possible'. In his letter the Minister listed four key issues for Dearing to review:

(a)   What is the scope for slimming down the curriculum itself?
(b)   What is the future of the 10-level scale for graduating children's attainments?
(c)   How the testing arrangements themselves can be simplified?
(d)   How can central administration of the National Curriculum and testing arrangements be improved?

John Patten's Cardiff speech marked a turning point in the history of the National Curriculum. He left the stage to polite applause and carrying an ATL T-shirt which, he said, would make a nice nightie for his young daughter Marie-Claire. The full text of his speech was hurriedly copied in a Cardiff print shop and immediately given to all Assembly members. The following morning, a resolution instructing the association's traditionally moderate Executive Committee to ballot members on limiting workload to an acceptable level was carried unanimously. The message had come too late. Patten's speech was long and badly structured, and the 'very important and detailed announcement' was drowned in a sea of rhetoric. His style of delivery was aloof and unsympathetic and he failed to capture his audience. As Patten left the stage, one Assembly member commented ruefully: 'He could at least have said sorry'. But at the time it was politically impossible for the Minister to apologize.

In a matter of months the three main teachers' unions, ATL, NASUWT and the NUT, were in industrial action. Each union was committed to supporting its members' resistance to undertake the 'unreasonable' workload arising from National Curriculum assessment and testing.

A new culture of consultation

From the moment of his appointment, Sir Ron Dearing exercised his power and his influence in a remarkable way. He was, after all, a skilled Whitehall operator, whose experience included working in several government departments including the Department of Trade and Industry (later the Department of Industry), and chairing the Post Office Corporation from 1981–7. His reputation was that of a straight-dealing, apolitical, teamwork man, having worked with ministers as politically diverse as Sir Keith Joseph and Tony Benn. In his previous role as Chairman of the HEFC he had merged the polytechnics' and universities' funding councils into a single body without causing waves, and he was well known for his diplomatic qualities and listening skills.

In terms of the policy process, Dearing's role fits almost perfectly that of a non-decision-maker. The process of non-decision-making is described by Bachrach and Baratz (1963) as 'the practice of limiting the scope of actual decision-making to "safe" issues by manipulating the dominant community values, myths, and political institutions and procedures'. Bachrach and Baratz argue that a non-decision-making situation can be said to exist 'when the dominant values, the accepted rules of the game, the existing power relations among groups, and the instruments of force, singly or in combination, effectively prevent certain grievances from developing into full-fledged issues which call for decisions'. Dearing has been the supreme gatekeeper, sticking closely to his original brief and ensuring that any 'debate' about the National Curriculum has been limited to a very specific purpose: essentially that of reduction and simplification. One non-negotiable ground-rule was firmly established at the outset: the 10-subject National Curriculum was 'A Good Thing'. There has been no real debate, only a massive (and indeed genuine) consultation exercise which has been contained within clearly defined boundaries. The scope for discussion has been limited to public consideration of issues which, though pressing in the short term, quite deliberately do not stimulate debate upon, or challenge, the principles on which the National Curriculum is based.

The faintest glimmer of the beginnings of an important new debate about the National Curriculum happened when *The Times Educational Supplement* published a provocative article by Nick Tate, at the time an Assistant Chief Executive at SCAA, headlined 'Off the fence on common culture' (*The Times Educational Supplement*, 29 July 1994). The article asked a question fundamental to any healthy and informed debate about a national curriculum: to what extent should such a curriculum reinforce a common culture and thus help a society to maintain its identity? Dr Tate stated that 'This is the key issue on which we [SCAA] seek a response.' However, this vital question about the extent to which a national curriculum should also be a nationalistic curriculum had not been included clearly and explicitly in each of the National Curriculum consultation questionnaires. Moreover, it was asked on the very day that the public consultation ended.

Dearing has proved to be strictly an 'art of the possible' man, never fighting a battle he cannot win. He has been powerful because it was his job to pull the government out of a crisis at a time when the National Curriculum was in a state of near-collapse and when there were signs that an industrial dispute could rumble on until the next election. Even though his wings were clipped, the government could not afford to ignore him and, so far at least, he has played ministers like a violin.

Dearing stories

Dearing set about his task in a characteristically businesslike, hard-working, but nevertheless friendly and open manner. He was eager to meet people, to exchange views, and to find out what others thought. His impact was immediate. Within a matter of weeks of his appointment, staff at the NCC and SEAC adopted what they called 'listening mode'. SCAA has followed suit, and the culture at Newcombe House (SCAA's London headquarters) is significantly more relaxed than that of its predecessors.

'Dearing stories' are now legion, but I have two personal favourites. The first happened on a train journey from London to York early in July 1993 when Dearing was drafting his interim report to the Secretary of State. We were both travelling to one of the many consultation conferences on the National Curriculum. We exchanged pleasantries and talked about the review. Among other things, I said the National Curriculum did not seem to take account of the fact that learning is a messy business. Much to my surprise, Sir Ron took my comment to heart and repeated it to the audience in York. He went on to include it in his interim report, where he states that achievement needs to be judged in the round rather than by reference to a closely specified definition expressed through detailed statements of attainment.

The second 'Dearing story' concerns the statement in his final report that the first priority for the 20 per cent discretionary time 'must' be to support work in the basics of literacy, oracy and numeracy in Key Stages 1 and 2. The issue was raised at one of a series of regular meetings between SCAA officials and representatives from the teachers' associations held on 11 January 1994. The point being made by the teachers' side was that the SCAA had no authority in law to tell teachers what they should teach in the so-called 'discretionary' time. Two days later, on 13 January, I received a letter from Sir Ron, which had been copied to Stewart Sutherland, then Her Majesty's Chief Inspector of Schools, explaining his use of the word 'must'. He says:

> As I was using the word, it was not intended as a command but as an expression of what teachers think is right, and my own personal confirmation of that judgement. But its force can be no more than to exhort. (I think Chris Woodhead, whose vocabulary is richer than mine, used the word 'hortatory' at the meeting.) And of course, for children who are doing well, there will be no need to use their time on the basics.

Putting to one side the argument that most primary teachers will concentrate on the basics whatever the law requires, this is yet another example of the fact that teachers, and their representative associations, were being listened to. The atmosphere had changed from one of 'well, a teachers' union would say that, wouldn't they' to 'that's a good idea, let's see what we can do with it'. A genuine culture of consultation had been established. At last, not only the teachers' associations, but the teaching profession as a whole was being taken seriously. The tragedy is that much of what is being said now has been said loudly and clearly by the teachers' associations, and by many others, for the past seven years – but until Dearing no one had been in 'listening mode'.

How has the National Curriculum changed?

Putting to one side the continual changes to the subject Orders which have undermined the credibility of the National Curriculum and increased teacher workloads, the basic framework of the ten foundation subjects remains more or less intact. In reality, information technology has been separated from the technology Order and has been given a life of its own.

The four key stages remain but, in effect, the National Curriculum ends at Key Stage 3. To correspond with this the 10-level scale has been truncated to 8 levels. There was, however, a catch. In spite of opposition from teachers' and subject associations, examination boards, schools (notably in the independent sector), and the views of the majority of respondents to Sir Ron Dearing's consultation (SCAA, 1994c), the SCAA chose to support those on the right who favour 'gilding the gold standard', until Gillian Shephard announced in 1995 that the 16–19 qualifications' framework should be reviewed by Ron Dearing as well. The outcome of this exercise remains to be seen. Where GCSE is concerned, the recent introduction of a starred grade as the highest level of achievement effectively downgrades the supremacy of the A grade and, by implication, all the other grades. In the new National Curriculum, rather than accepting Level 8 as the highest level of achievement, SCAA has introduced a level for 'exceptional perfor-mance' for each attainment target in all the foundation subjects. These were immediately dubbed 'SCAARED As' by the teachers' associations, who pointed out that the new levels would be demotivating for pupils (Level 8, equivalent to a GCSE Grade B, is an exceptional achievement for a 14-year-old) and misleading for parents. The SCAA is unable to explain to what problem the new 'exceptional performance' level is a solution. At the other end of the spectrum, for Levels 1–3, the SCAA has not yet arrived at a way of recording the very considerable achievements of large numbers of pupils with special educational needs, some of whom may spend their entire school career working towards Level 1. This surely tells us something about the Authority's priorities in shaping an entitlement curriculum which allows all pupils to experience success.

Serious doubts remain about whether, as SCAA intends, it will be possible to teach the National Curriculum and RE within 80 per cent of the recommended minimum weekly teaching time at Key Stages 1, 2 and 3, and within 60 per cent at Key Stage 4. The curriculum is still not under control, and reducing it from 120–130 per cent to 90–100 per cent does not solve the problem of overload and may intensify prescription in practice. Of particular concern is Key Stage 2. This is the longest and, with the possible exception of Key Stage 4, the most problematic and 'overweight' (at least from the teachers' viewpoint) of the four key stages. Key Stage 2 teachers have made heroic efforts to teach the nine-subject curriculum to classes of 30 plus covering the full ability range. As one teacher described it, managing the National Curriculum at Key Stage 2 is like 'eating the elephant bit by bit' (Rosemary Webb, 1993). There has been much talk of specialist and semi-specialist teaching at this key stage, and much concern about trimming and diluting the curriculum to manageable proportions. All this neatly evades a central, but unpalatable, fact: teachers and schools will continue to encounter genuine problems in covering the whole of the National Curriculum at Key Stage 2 until such a time as primary schools (and particularly Years 4–6) are resourced in a way that is truly compatible with the secondary system, allowing for genuine specialist provision. The problem of securing curriculum continuity between primary and secondary schools will remain until the resourcing issue is properly addressed.

The real debate about Key Stage 4 has barely begun. Dearing's final report states that the National Curriculum should take up 60 per cent of curriculum time at this key stage. But what happens with the remaining 40 per cent remains unclear. The debate about short courses rages on, and firm proposals on development of vocational pathways are slow to emerge, in spite of the fact that Dearing has been working closely with NCVQ on the piloting of Part I GNVQs for 14–16-year-olds.

Other issues hang in the air. Only time will tell the extent to which the statutory tests are to be based on the curriculum and how what is taught will change to match the tests, rather than *vice versa*. It is unclear how the SCAA and the DFEE intend to handle the absurdity in secondary schools in which for three years pupils are assessed by levels, and then switch to A*–G grades for GCSE. It is difficult to see how value-added league tables can be developed if the two systems are used.

Wales has all but declared UDI, and the Curriculum Cymreig (the Welsh version of the National Curriculum) is firmly taking root. The Northern Ireland Curriculum is based on six areas of study and six educational themes. In Scotland, where the curriculum is non-statutory, the 5–14 Development Programme covers five broad areas, each with a recommended minimum time allocation; and plans have been announced for a new unified framework of courses and awards for the final two years of secondary education.

The United Kingdom has four separate curricula. The legal force of the National Curriculum does not apply to schools in the independent sector, nor to city technology colleges. The National Curriculum, as originally envisaged, has become a curriculum for those between the ages of 5 to 14 in maintained schools in England, from which some children with special educational needs can be disapplied. The concept of an elementary school curriculum has been re-invented.

The teachers' associations and the National Curriculum

From the inception of the NCC and SEAC there have been regular (usually termly) meetings between representatives from the six main teachers' associations and senior officials from the two Councils. The tradition has continued with SCAA. The meetings serve three main purposes.

First, and most important, they have allowed a dialogue to be established between Council/Authority officials and the teachers' associations. The latter are able to submit agenda items and, where appropriate, papers for discussion at the meetings. Over time, it became custom and practice for appropriate Council officials to join the meetings and address particular agenda items. The teachers' associations have been able to build upon these very useful contacts in developing sound, collaborative working relationships with the staff of each Council and subsequently with officials at SCAA.

Second, the meetings provide a welcome opportunity for representatives from the teachers' associations to meet together on a regular basis and share ideas. (This might not, of course, been seen as highly desirable by the government.) Each association is usually represented by two people, and the pre-meetings are used to discuss agenda items, talk through points of agreement and differences, and to decide what needed to be said, and who was going to 'front' each agenda item. Working relationships between representatives of the teachers' associations have been enhanced, and there has always been a healthy – and often humorous – respect for the differences of opinion which are bound to exist.

Third, the meetings have provided a valuable opportunity to forge links with colleagues in the independent sector. Representatives from, for example, the Girls' School Association, the Headmasters' Conference, and the Independent Association of Preparatory Schools also attended the meetings. In time these colleagues were to become some of the most outspoken critics of aspects of the National Curriculum and thus strong allies of their counterparts in the maintained sector.

There has always been a downside to the meetings. There was rarely any strong indication that the views expressed by the teachers' side were being formally communicated to members of the two Councils or to SCAA. From the outset it was clear that the political agenda was being drawn up elsewhere and that, increasingly, many Council members had more interesting – and more problematic – political fish to fry. The teachers' side asked for minutes of the meetings to be included as an agenda item for Council/Authority meetings, but there is no evidence that this has happened. The reason usually given was that the Councils/Authority had far too many papers to deal with anyway. David Pascall only once made an appearance at a meeting in York, but colleagues agreed afterwards that we had been talked 'at' rather than 'to'.

The English fiasco

In the early autumn of 1992, and at the initiative of Michael Barber, then Assistant Secretary for Education at the NUT, education officials from the six main teachers' associations met in London to look in more detail at curriculum and assessment issues. Spurred on by the proposals in the White Paper *Choice and Diversity*, it was important to explore how we could ensure that our effective working relationship with the two Councils – particularly with the NCC – could be maintained and developed with the newly proposed SCAA.

An agenda was drawn up and the first meeting was held at Hamilton House in London in September 1992. However, the formal agenda was overtaken by events. The NCC had just advised the Secretary of State that the National Curriculum English Order should be reviewed. The group was outraged and questioned the genuineness of the so-called consultation meetings with the NCC. At these meetings, the point had been made time and again that of all the National Curriculum Orders, English was least in need of revision. The Order was by no means perfect (what English Order could be?) but there were more important tasks to tackle, not least in terms of revising – and possibly temporarily suspending – the technology Order. Teachers were becoming restless and were already beginning to question the credibility of the National Curriculum. Chopping and changing the Orders should have happened only where absolutely necessary. This was not, we considered, the case with English. To add insult to injury, the NCC's advice to the Secretary of State was based, in part, on publicly funded research, commissioned by the NCC and conducted by Bridie Raban at the University of Warwick, which – as seemed custom and practice at the time – was not in the public domain.

The group worked intensively on the text of a draft letter to David Pascall, which was sent in the name of Barry Hilditch of the Secondary Heads' Association, at that time chairman of the group. In the event, the revision of the English Order went ahead, but not before a number of points had been strongly, and firmly, made.

The St William's College meeting, September 1992

On 30 September 1992 an advisory group of nine people comprising representatives from the teachers' associations and the independent sector met with Chris Woodhead, then Chief Executive of the NCC, Jenny Hall, an Assistant Chief Executive (in her time a linchpin between the NCC and the teachers' associations) and Tim Cornford, the Council's Director of Publications and Information, at St William's College in York. The advisory group had been set up to consider the role of teachers in revising the National Curriculum. However, the first task of the meeting was to focus on the review of the English Order. The teachers' side reaffirmed concern about the reasons for, and the timing of, the review, and questioned the evidence base upon which the Order was to be revised. The discussion was heated and, at moments, extremely angry. One of our chief concerns was that the NCC should focus on wider issues of content and overload, and on an overall approach to reviewing and revising the National Curriculum Orders. Meddling with an English Order for political purposes could, we said, do nothing but harm. At times like this it seemed that the NCC was more concerned with throwing the occasional lamb chop to right-wingers (in this case, in the shape of grammar, punctuation and spelling) than with teachers' views on the English Order as a whole.

The discussion on English came to an end. While the situation had not been amicably resolved, feelings had been well and truly aired. At that juncture in the meeting it seemed essential that we should move on to a more positive agenda and identify ways in which the teachers' organizations could genuinely influence policy rather than continue to engage in what was in danger of becoming a ritual of (highly justified) complaint.

Attention then focused on devising a framework for reviewing the National Curriculum. At the 1992 NCC/Teachers' Associations' summer conference (which has since become an annual event) the NUT had produced a paper on the role of teachers in revising the National Curriculum. It was agreed that this would form the basis of a strategy paper that could be considered by the Council. It was essential that the paper was one which Chris Woodhead and David Pascall could not only live with, but actually support. Michael Barber agreed to develop the document in consultation with the other teachers' associations for consideration by the Council in December of that year. It was confirmed that the document needed to be acceptable and workable for both the teachers' associations and the NCC.

The six union document

Work proceeded apace on what became known as the six union document. Those directly involved in drafting the document were Michael Barber of the NUT, Arthur de Caux of the NAHT, Barry Hilditch from SHA, Henry Iven from NASUWT, Jackie Miller from PAT and myself from ATL. We were all unequivocally clear from previous experience that working together on joint ventures is a time-consuming business. It was therefore essential to stick to the knitting and target our efforts very precisely. The work was undertaken in a powerfully collaborative climate and the unity of the group's collective thinking was revealed in our responses to the various drafts.

In the first instance the intended audience had been the NCC and it was for this reason that the document focused on a review of the curriculum. However, the impending creation of SCAA made it necessary to address assessment issues as well, as a result of which the original draft was considerably expanded. The jointly drafted document *A Framework for Reviewing the National Curriculum* (Joint Teachers' Associations, 1993) was completed in April 1993. It was endorsed by the National Association of Teachers in Further and Higher Education (NATFHE) and by the five major organizations representing schools in the independent sector. The document was despatched to Sir Ron Dearing immediately he took up appointment as Chairman of the NCC and SEAC under cover of a letter signed by the general secretary of each of the six main teachers' organizations. On the same day, a joint press statement from the six organizations announced: 'Reviewing the National Curriculum: Six Teacher Organisations Speak With One Voice'.

What followed is now history. The six general secretaries met with Sir Ron Dearing and presented their case. Sir Ron listened attentively. Further meetings with the teachers' associations, both joint and bilateral, ensued. Sir Ron then set about reviewing the National Curriculum Orders very much along the lines set down in the document. He has, as the document requested, provided effective mechanisms for professional input and confirmed that any revisions will be based on a wide range of publicly available evidence. Most important, he has made a public commitment that SCAA will not tamper with the new National Curriculum Orders for five years from the time of their introduction in September 1995. The collaborative climate, with the education officials from the teachers' associations working efficiently, effectively and purposefully together, resulted in what is, with hindsight, a remarkable achievement. It is only regrettable that subsequent industrial action over National Curriculum workloads has caused rifts between the teachers' associations which may take many years to heal.

Future collaboration with SCAA

Over the past five or six years the teachers' associations have devoted much time, and a considerable amount of hard work, to influencing the policy process both separately and together. This has included the joint meetings with the NCC, the SEAC and, more recently, with the SCAA. These meetings are usually good-humoured (perhaps too much so) but at times it has seemed that they are in danger of becoming a necessary, but somewhat tedious, ritual, regarded with a degree of cynicism on all sides. The truth of the matter is that everyone (and not just teachers) is suffering from innovation fatigue. Time and again we have returned to the same questions – for example, curriculum manageability at Key Stage 2, cross-curricular themes, the technology Order and the 14–19 curriculum. Time and again we were either stonewalled or politely told that it would all come out in the wash – or words to that effect. Precisely whose wash was never made clear.

The most productive joint meetings have been those set up to focus on a specific issue. If valuable time (on all sides) is not to be wasted, it is essential that future meetings have a clear focus and that the teachers' side is well prepared. Without such a focus, and without the necessary preparation, there is a serious danger that the meetings between SCAA and the teachers' associations will become a time-consuming but fruitless talking shop. If they hope to be taken seriously, it is for the teachers' associations to put their collective house in order, sort out their differences on testing and assessment, and to consider, collectively and strategically, how best they can influence education policy. All this, of course, is very much easier said than done, but continued tensions between the unions, eagerly exploited by the government and, of course, by the media, can only do harm to teachers and discredit the teaching profession as a whole.

The teachers' associations and research

Common sense suggests that any organization embarking on an experiment of the size, scope and the cost to the public purse, of the National Curriculum should be responsible for monitoring, reviewing and evaluating progress. To some extent this task has been undertaken by OFSTED. But important aspects of this work, such as costing out resource implications, measuring teachers' workload and monitoring curriculum manageability, have been neglected. Much of this work has been left to the teachers' associations which, over the past five years, have commissioned key research projects to evaluate the effects of the National Curriculum (see, for example, Campbell and Neill, 1990, 1992, 1993, 1994a; Campbell *et al.*, 1991; Coopers and Lybrand Deloitte, 1991; NASUWT, 1990, 1991; Osborne and Black, 1993; Shorrocks *et al.*, 1993; Rosemary Webb 1993, 1994). It has been the teachers themselves who have begun to accept and acknowledge that they are engaged in a national experiment and it is teachers and their unions who have been key players in monitoring and evaluating the outcomes of that experiment.

What follows is the story of just one piece of research. This is not to say that the study described here is any more, or less, important than any others. It is used here to illustrate how research commissioned by one of the teachers' associations in direct response to teachers' concerns expressed about unmanageable workloads had a significant influence upon public policy. The research legitimized teachers' concerns, gave the teaching workforce a powerful voice and provided hard evidence about curriculum overload.

In 1989, when pallet-loads of National Curriculum documents were arriving in schools, the AMMA, as it then was, commissioned researchers at Warwick University to undertake a one-year study of teacher work-loads at Key Stage 1. The Association wanted clear evidence, rooted in fact rather than rhetoric, about the amount of time infant teachers were spending on work, and how they were spending it. Five years on, the research was described in *Curriculum Reform At Key Stage 1: Teacher Commitment and Policy Failure* (Campbell and Neill, 1994a). The book provides a catalogue of evidence of the reforms of the curriculum and its assessment at Key Stage 1 in England and Wales as they were phased in serially from autumn 1989, with all the foundation subjects being in statutory Orders by autumn 1992.

At the outset of National Curriculum implementation, AMMA was seriously concerned about the number of infant teachers who were struggling to find ways of coping with the workload imposed upon them. There was a worrying increase in the letters, telephone calls and casework enquiries from infant teachers, many desperate for help. In the first year of the research, ninety-five Key Stage 1 teachers logged the time they spent on work for fourteen consecutive days on a specially designed record sheet, the Record of Teacher Time (ROTT). Teacher time does not exist in a vacuum insulated from education policy, especially on the delivery of the curriculum. The research was deliberately designed to identify issues arising from current policy. Although it was widely claimed that, following the implementation of the National Curriculum, teachers were having to spend considerably more time than previously on their work, there was little hard evidence. The last major study of English primary schoolteachers' work, *The Teacher's Day* (Hilsum and Cane, 1971) had been published nearly twenty years earlier and referred to junior teachers only.

The first year of the study, reported in *Thirteen Hundred and Thirty Days* (Campbell and Neill, 1990), showed an average working week of just under 50 hours, with some teachers working up to 70 hours. The use of teacher time, with more hours devoted to non-teaching activities than to teaching itself, represented a significant shift from the position in 1971, when junior teachers spent 58 per cent of their time on teaching and 42 per cent on non-teaching tasks. The response from Duncan Graham, then Chairman and Chief Executive of the NCC, was harsh and abrasive. Speaking at an AMMA education conference on the day the first study was published, Graham criticized the Association for 'going in a bit too much for the gloom and doom' and for 'creating the impression that everybody was doing a 70 hour slog' (AMMA, 1990). The response from education ministers was equally predictable: teachers were resistant to change, next year things would settle down and workloads would become more manageable. Concerns about workload and manageability were a blip, not a bleep.

Not convinced, AMMA asked the researchers to monitor progress in 1991. The findings of the second year, summarized in *Workloads, Achievements and Stress* (Campbell *et al.*, 1991) do not support the 'blip theory'. The objective data provided a typical working week of around 54 hours, with Year 2 teachers (who are responsible for the statutory tests) working around 58 hours. The 1991 study had an additional, qualitative dimension: as well as asking teachers for facts, they were also asked about feelings. As the researchers point out, without the effort, stress and commitment from teachers, the reform process would not have been possible.

Two further studies led to *Teacher Time and Curriculum Manageability at Key Stage 1* (Campbell and Neill, 1992) and *Four Years On: The Failure of Curriculum Reform at Key Stage 1* (Campbell and Neill, 1993). Teachers' working hours were little changed from previous years, with a small increase in overall time. Infant teachers were working over 50 hours a week on average, with one in ten working more than 60 hours. The researchers also calculated a teaching:preparation ratio of 1:0.9. For every hour of teaching carried out, the teachers spent a further 54 minutes on preparation.

In the last year of the study the teachers gave their views on how the implementation of the National Curriculum and RE had affected curriculum standards, teachers' skills and professionalism. In science, technology, history and geography there was a marked perception that standards had been raised. In the teaching of reading, art, PE, music, RE and other teaching the perceived impact was lowered standards. Although planning with colleagues and assessing pupils' learning were seen as having improved by most of the teachers, 40 per cent of them thought that their skills in catering for pupils with special educational needs had been damaged. Almost half the teachers thought the sense of their own professionalism had been damaged, with only 17 per cent thinking it had been enhanced. As Campbell and Neill point out, teachers did not subvert educational policy. On the contrary, they did their best to implement it. However, the research provided first-hand evidence that the curriculum put into statute was unmanageable and would not fit into the time available. The assessment and testing arrangements reflected purposes widely seen as conflicting and contradictory. Most important, no one other than the teachers' unions tried to cost out the implications for teachers' working lives.

It is over six years since this work was first commissioned. The research, together with a one-year study of secondary teachers' workloads which was also commissioned by AMMA, led to the Teaching As Work Project at the University of Warwick, where Campbell and Neill recorded and analysed nearly 7,000 working days from over 700 teachers over the period between 1990 and 1992 in England, Wales, Northern Ireland and the Channel Islands. It has provided data which contributed to evidence for three further books (Campbell and Neill 1994b, 1994c; Campbell *et al.*, 1994) and numerous articles, and the findings have been widely reported in the press, and on radio and television. Evidence from the research has been quoted in parliamentary debates and used by Sir Ron Dearing in making his case for slimming down the National Curriculum. The study also led the STRB to conduct a large-scale, national survey of teachers' working time.

In the autumn of 1995 the slimmed-down National Curriculum Orders were taught in schools for the first time. What is urgently needed is a firm assurance from SCAA that the Authority will monitor and evaluate the 'new' National Curriculum from the very first day of its implementation in September 1995, and that evidence from such an evaluation will be in the public domain. With all the cutting and pasting, there is still no guarantee that the new Orders will be more manageable than the old ones. Two things are certain: it will take time for the new Orders to take root in the classroom; and it will take time to develop high-quality national tests and statutory teacher assessment to match the detail of the new level descriptions against which performance is assessed. The first stage of the National Curriculum experiment was a national disaster. Teachers have yet to be fully persuaded that there is a genuine commitment on the part of government – and in particular on the part of the Secretary of State for Education Gillian Shephard – to get it right the second time around.

SCAA has a key role to play in addressing resourcing and manageability issues and in promoting clearly targeted research and development initiatives. The Authority is required by law to 'keep under review all aspects of the curriculum ... and all aspects of school examinations and assessment' and to 'advise the Secretary of State on such matters concerned with the curriculum ... as they may see fit' (Education Act 1993, Section 245). This remit must surely include advising the Secretary of State on issues concerning resourcing and manageability. Although the Authority has publicly acknowledged problems created by curriculum overload, it has produced neither evidence nor advice on resourcing issues. Alongside its responsibility for designing the National Curriculum, SCAA should be called upon to provide clear, unambiguous evidence, based on independent research, of the resource implications of the National Curriculum. Moreover, the Authority, along with the STRB, needs to take seriously the issue of teachers' workloads and demonstrate how, under current levels of resourcing, all elements of the statutorily imposed curriculum (including, for example, religious education, sex education and, of course, the National Curriculum) can be taught and assessed efficiently and effectively in a variety of school contexts to classes of upwards of thirty children. Put bluntly, the job needs to be properly planned, costed and tested. A rushed slimming down of the statutory Orders is not, of itself, evidence that the new curriculum will be any more coherent and manageable than the old one. The proof of the curriculum pudding will be in the teaching and learning that goes on in the classroom, not in the cutting and pasting that went on beforehand. By commissioning independent research, teachers and their associations have played a critical role in monitoring the implementation of national education policy and influencing its development. They should not, however, be expected to do the work of a government that is either too arrogant or too cowardly properly to cost, monitor and appraise its own, massively expensive, 'reform' programme.

After the deluge

Education history is being made at what seems like an unprecedented pace. It is too early to take stock of the full impact of recent education legislation on teachers, schools and on pupils, but the headline 'After the Deluge' fits neatly. It feels just about right to describe this point in history in this way. It is also the title of ATL-commissioned research into the impact of recent education legislation on roles and responsibilities in primary schools (Rosemary Webb, 1994). The deluge of directives – not least the endless outpourings from the DFEE and SCAA – has slowed down. Arguments about change, and indeed about consolidation, are becoming more rational, and are no longer based upon ministerial whim or Government diktat. Teachers have been promised five years of curriculum stability – an opportunity for the profession to catch its breath, to focus less intensely on the detail of curriculum content and to concentrate instead on a much more important issue: the endlessly complex business of teaching and learning. There is, at last, space for the intellectual side of the debate to open up, for discussions about pedagogy (a corner of the curriculum garden that is still relatively secret) to be rekindled, and for the teaching profession to be re-energized.

The effects of the National Curriculum have not been wholly negative, and professional commitment has not been entirely dissipated. There remains a broad consensus on its structural benefits, and it is seen as providing for progression and continuity and, with careful design and monitoring, as a potential source of coherence. Teachers are working more collaboratively, although Rosemary Webb (1994) points to tensions between the increased co-operation among staff and the promotion of directive management styles which 'undermine the feasibility and credibility of teachers working together collegially to formulate policies and promote continuity of practice'. If a national curriculum is genuinely to raise overall standards, stretch pupils' abilities and help create generations of articulate, confident and enthusiastic learners, then surely it needs to be a growing, changing, dynamic organism – not just a bureaucrat's dream of rigid ring-binders, pretty portfolios or tidy tickboxes. As (the then Conservative and now Labour) MP Alan Howarth wrote when challenging the notion of cultural authoritarianism and the 'Little Englanders' who are gunning for teachers: 'A curriculum should always be provisional and exploratory. In our study of English and history our idea of ourselves as a community is continuously renewed. There will always be those who fear this process. But education, like politics, should be characterised by generosity' (The *Guardian*, 15 October 1994, 'English as she will be spoken'). The idea of an exploratory, generous curriculum has immediate appeal. But how do we get there from here?

First and foremost, SCAA will need to establish structural mechanisms whereby teachers, their subject organizations and their unions are welcomed into the ongoing debate on the curriculum, rather than brought in at a moment's notice to help resolve a crisis. Given the diversity of the profession, and the wealth of ideas about the curriculum, teaching and learning, it can hardly be expected that teachers will speak with one voice. We must learn to acknowledge differences and thrive on diversity. Channels of communication must be opened up: the debate on the curriculum must continue.

Too often in recent years, much of the criticism of the National Curriculum has focused on the practical problems created by its implementation. We need to consider whether the National Curriculum as we understand it is not only impracticable, but also fundamentally misconceived. We must continue to ask questions about the worth of the curriculum, as well as its practicability; about its ends as well as its means. It is surely the responsibility of all concerned with curriculum development – including teachers, those in higher education, teachers' unions, subject associations and, of course, SCAA – to help open up the debate. Indeed, it is here that SCAA has a key role to play. The danger is that, having sorted out the chaos of the original National Curriculum Orders, the temptation will be for the Authority to slip into the background, adopt a low profile, and keep the National Curriculum more or less ticking over. This would be a waste of an opportunity. The time is right to look again at the potential of the National Curriculum and to explore how best it can be used to create a sense of public ownership of education and raise the status of teaching and schooling.

A sensible start would be to remind teachers and schools that there are alternatives. Section 16 of the 1988 ERA allows for development work and experiments within the curriculum and, with the permission of the Secretary of State, the National Curriculum can be disapplied or modified. As an essential part of any future research and development work, SCAA must surely encourage schools to think for themselves, provide support and encouragement to teachers wishing to develop curriculum initiatives, and disseminate examples of curriculum innovation. It is worth hanging on to the original idea of a 'framework' rather than a 'strait-jacket' and encouraging schools to explore the concept of curriculum subsidiarity within an overall national framework or structure.

If we have learnt nothing else from the past seven years, one thing is certain: manufacturing a crisis in education, followed by the imposition of untested reforms backed by statutory force, is not the way to get the best out of schools, teachers or pupils. As Campbell (Campbell and Neill, 1994a) shows, such an approach is profoundly detrimental to teachers' sense of their own professionalism and counter-productive for the reforms. In the long term, the solution lies not in statutory instruments and government circulars, but in schools and with teachers. It is teachers who, through their ingenuity and sheer hard work, have found ways of coping with the National Curriculum. And it is schools which, almost in spite of the National Curriculum, have held on to and fought for beliefs about their primary purpose: creating the best possible environment for learning. If politicians are genuinely to regain the confidence of the professionals, they must trust teachers to do their best. For some this will be an act of faith. But if schools are to survive and flourish in a climate of constant change, the spotlight must be on schools as communities of learners, thinking through and resolving problems for themselves, and constantly challenging conventional wisdom. At the end of the day, schools will need to find their own salvation.

Two more things need to be said. The first concerns the need for planned change. Civil servants at the DFEE need look no further than a publication by HM Treasury (HMSO, 1991), intended for use by all government departments, for a step-by-step guide to appraisal. The guide suggests that the sequence should begin early in the gestation of any expenditure proposal. It suggests the following:

(a) define the objectives;
(b) consider the options;
(c) identify, quantify and, where possible, value the costs, benefits and uncertainties of each option;
(d) put those costs and benefits which can be valued in money terms on a comparable basis;
(e) weigh up the uncertainties;
(f) assess the balance between options;
(g) present the results.

It is worth stressing that this has been written specifically for those advising policy-makers, and for policy-makers themselves. Had the guidance been heeded throughout the implementation of the National Curriculum, many hundreds and thousands of pounds from the public purse (estimates of the total costs of implementing the National Curriculum stretch to over £750 million) need not have been squandered.

The second and final point concerns the cost in human terms. Many resources have been wasted since the introduction of the National Curriculum, but the biggest waste of all has been of teachers, disillusioned and demoralized by the demands that unsupported change has made on them. The ultimate tragedy of the National Curriculum is the sheer waste of professional lives. Too many wise, talented and experienced teachers have left the profession exhausted and embittered, with a profound sense of despair and a painful experience of failure, rather than with a feeling of achievement, pride, dignity and self-respect. Such waste is unnecessary and, ultimately, unforgivable.

*   *   *

* I am most grateful to Paul Black, Jim Campbell, Clyde Chitty, Tim Cornford, Paul McGill, Ian Langtry and Peter Smith who commented on early drafts for me. I should also like to thank Midge Blake, Rosa Drohomirecka and Janet Manning, who, between them, comprise ATL's Communications Department, for providing the nearest thing to a human thesaurus. Finally, many thanks go to colleagues in ATL's Policy Unit, and in particular to Meryl Thompson for her invaluable support and encouragement, and for helping to untangle ideas for this chapter.

Postscript

Nothing stands still. This chapter was first drafted in the Summer of 1994 and much has happened since. So far as the National Curriculum is concerned, we are entering a phase of relative stability. Meanwhile, the debate on national assessment is beginning to open up, and not before time. A national framework for the under-fives curriculum has been drawn up by SCAA, and Sir Ron Dearing is about to report on the 16–19 qualifications' framework. To his credit, Dr Nick Tate, Chief Executive of SCAA, has initiated a series of national and international conferences on wider aspects of the curriculum. Lessons have been learnt from the past and we must continue to look to the future, but this time with one eye firmly fixed on reality.

Sheila Dainton
January 1996

Bibliography

Aldrich, R. (1988), 'The National Curriculum: an Historical Perspective', in Lawton, D. and Chitty, C. (eds), *The National Curriculum*, Bedford Way Paper 33, Institute of Education, University of London.

AMMA (1987), *Digest of the Government's Consultation Papers and AMMA's Comments*, London: AMMA (now ATL).

AMMA (1990), *National Curriculum Key Stages 1–3: The Continuing Debate*, Education Conference Report, London: AMMA (now ATL).

ATL (1993), *Assembly 1993 – Proceedings*, London: ATL.

Auld, R. (1976), Report on William Tyndale Junior School, London: ILEA.

Bachrach, P. and Baratz, M. (1963), 'Decisions and Nondecisions: An Analytical Framework', *American Political Science Review*, 57. Quoted in Ham, C. and Hill, M. (1984), *The Policy Process in the Modern Capitalist State*, Sussex: Wheatsheaf.

Baker, K. (1993), *The Turbulent Years*, London: Faber and Faber.

Barber, M. (1992), *Education and the Teacher Unions*, London: Cassell.

Barber, M. (1994), *The Making of the 1944 Education Act*, London: Cassell.

Barber, M. (1994b), Article in *The Times*, 7 January 1994, London: Times Newspapers.

Barber, M. and Graham, D. (1992), *Sense, Nonsense and the National Curriculum*, London: Falmer.

Black, P. (1992), 'The Shifting Scenery of the National Curriculum', in O'Hear, P. and White, J. (eds), *Assessing the National Curriculum*, London: Paul Chapman Publishing.

Board of Education (1941), *Education after the War* (Green Book), London: HMSO.

Board of Education (1943), *Curriculum and Examinations in Secondary School* (The Norwood Report), London: HMSO.

Bolton, E. (1994a), 'Alternative Education Policies: School Inspection', in IPPR/Rivers Oram Press.

Bolton, E. (1994b), 'Initial Teacher Training – The Reforms', in *Report*, Vol. 17, No. 1, London: ATL.

Bowe, R. and Ball, S. (1992), *Reforming Education and Changing Schools*, London: Routledge.

Butler, R. A. (1971), *The Art of the Possible*, London: Hamish Hamilton.

Campbell, R. and Neill, S. (1990), *Thirteen Hundred and Thirty Days: Final*

Report of a Pilot Study of Teacher Time at Key Stage 1, London: AMMA (now ATL).

Campbell, R. and Neill, S. (1992), *Teacher Time and Curriculum Manageability at Key Stage 1*, London: AMMA (now ATL).

Campbell, R. and Neill, S. (1993), *Four Years On: The Failure of Curriculum Reform at Key Stage 1*, London: ATL.

Campbell, R. and Neill, S. (1994a), *Curriculum Reform at Key Stage 1: Teacher Commitment and Policy Failure*, Harlow: ATL/Longman.

Campbell, R. and Neill, S. (1994b), *Primary Teachers at Work*. London: Routledge.

Campbell, R. and Neill, S. (1994c), *Secondary Teachers at Work*. London: Routledge.

Campbell, R. *et al.* (1991), *Workloads, Achievement and Stress*, London: AMMA (now ATL).

Campbell, R. *et al.* (1994), *The Meaning of Infant Teachers' Work*, London: Routledge.

Central Advisory Council for Education (1967), *Children and their Primary Schools* (The Plowden Report), London: HMSO.

Chitty, C. (ed.) (1993), *The National Curriculum: Is it Working?* Harlow: Longman.

Coopers and Lybrand Deloitte (1991), *Costs of the National Curriculum in Primary Schools*, commissioned by the National Union of Teachers, London: NUT.

Cox, Brian (1992), *The Great Betrayal: Memoirs of a Life in Education*, London: Chapman.

Cox, C. B. and Dyson, A. E. (eds) (1971), *The Black Papers on Education*, a revised edition.

Dearing, R. (1993), *The National Curriculum and its Assessment: Interim Report*, York and London: NCC and SEAC.

Dearing, R. (1994), *The National Curriculum and its Assessment: Final Report*, London: SCAA.

DES (1977), *Education in Schools: A Consultative Document* (cmnd 6869), London: HMSO.

DES (1979), *Aspects of Secondary Education in England: An HMI Report*, London: HMSO.

DES (1985), *Better Schools*, London: HMSO.

DES/The Welsh Office (1987), *National Curriculum Task Group on Assessment and Testing: A Report*, London: DES.

DES/Welsh Office (1987), *The National Curriculum 5–16*, a Consultative Document, London: DES.

DES (1987), *The National Curriculum: A Consultative Document*, London: HMSO.

DES (1988a), *Task Group on Assessment and Testing: A Report*, London: HMSO.

DES (1988b), *Task Group on Assessment and Testing: Three Supplementary Reports*, London: HMSO.

DES (1989a), *Circular 5/89*, London: HMSO.

DES (1989b), *National Curriculum: From Policy to Practice*, London: HMSO.

Dewey, J. (1916), *Education and Democracy*, New York: The Free Press.

DFE (1992), *Choice and Diversity: a new framework for schools*, London: HMSO.

DFE (1993), *DFE Review – A Plan for Action*, London: DFE.

Education Act 1993, London: HMSO.

Education Act 1994, London: HMSO.

Education (Schools) Act 1992, London: HMSO.

Education Reform Act 1988, London: HMSO.

Further and Higher Education Act 1992, London: HMSO.

Gipps, C. (1988), 'National Assessment – TGAT for Teachers', article in *NUT Education Review*, Autumn 1988.

Graham, D. and Tytler, D. (1993), *A Lesson for Us All*, London: Routledge.

Ham, C. and Hill, M. (1984), *The Policy Process in the Modern Capitalist State*, Sussex: Wheatsheaf.

Hargreaves, D. (1994), *The Mosaic of Learning*, London: Demos.

Haviland, J. (1988), *Take Care, Mr Baker!* London: Fourth Estate.

Hewton, E. (1986), *Education in Recession*, London: Allen and Unwin.

HMSO (1991), *Economic Appraisal in Central Government: A Technical Guide for Government Departments*, London: HMSO.

Hilsum, S. and Cane, B. (1971), *The Teacher's Day*, Slough: NFER.

Joint Teachers' Associations (1993), *A Framework for Reviewing the National Curriculum*, London: Joint Teachers' Associations.

Kogan, M. (1971), *The Politics of Education*, Middlesex: Penguin.

Marenbon, J. (1993), *Testing Time: The Dearing Review and the Future of the National Curriculum*, London: Centre for Policy Studies.

MacGregor, J. (1990), Speech to AMMA Assembly in *Proceedings of AMMA Assembly 1990*, London: AMMA (now ATL).

Maclure, S. (1988), *Education Re-formed*, Kent: Hodder and Stoughton.

Moon, R., Murphy, P., and Raynor, J. (eds) (1989), *Policies for the Curriculum*, London: Hodder and Stoughton.

NASUWT (1990), *Teacher Time Survey*, Birmingham: NASUWT.

NASUWT (1991), *Teacher Time Survey*, Birmingham: NASUWT.

NCC (1990), *Curriculum Guidance 3: The Whole Curriculum*, York: NCC.

NCC (1991), *The National Curriculum Corporate Plan 1992–1995*, York: NCC.

NCC (1992), *The National Curriculum: An Overview of the Cross-Curricular Themes* (unpublished).

NCC (1993), *Spiritual and Moral Development – A Discussion Paper*, York: NCC.

NUT (1985), *Response to Better Schools*, London: NUT.

NUT (1992), *Miss, the Rabbit Ate the Floating Apple: An Evaluation of the KS1 Tests*, London: NUT.

Osborne, M. and Black, E. (1994), *Developing the National Curriculum at*

Key Stage 2: The Changing Nature of Teachers' Work, Birmingham: NASUWT.

Ozga, J., and Lawn, M. (1981), *Teachers, Professionalism and Class*, Lewes: Falmer.

Pascall, D. (1992), *Speech to Cambridgeshire Primary Headteachers*, London: NCC Press Release.

Pascall, D. (1992), 'Standards in Religious Education', paper presented to the Association of Religious Education Advisers and Inspectors, University of Keele (July).

Pascall, D. (1993), 'Setting the Agenda for Primary Education', paper presented to Junior Education Conference, Oxford Brookes University (March).

Plaskow, M. (ed) (1985), *The life and Death of the Schools' Council*, Lewes: Falmer.

Pollard, A. *et al.* (1994), *Changing English Primary Schools? The Impact of the Education Reform Act at Key Stage 1*, London: Cassell.

Popper, K. (1945), *The Open Society and its Enemies*. Quoted in Hargreaves, D. (1994), *The Mosaic of Learning*, London: Demos.

Rumbold, A. (1987), Response to Miss Fookes, transcript of Standing Committee J, 17 December.

Sayer, J. (1993), *The Future Governance of Education*, London: Cassell.

SCAA (1994a), *Religious Education: Model Syllabuses – The Legal Requirement* (page 3), London: SCAA.

SCAA (1994b), *National Curriculum Subject Draft Proposals and Overview Document*, London, SCAA.

SCAA (1994c), *The Review of the National Curriculum – A Report on the 1994 Consultation*, London: SCAA.

School Teachers' Pay and Conditions Act 1991, London: HMSO.

SEAC (1992), *An evaluation of the KS1 Tests 1991*, Diane Shorrocks *et al.*, Leeds University, London: SEAC.

Shorrocks, D. *et al.* (1993), *Testing and Assessing 6 and 7 Year Olds: The Evaluation of the 1992 Key Stage 1 National Curriculum Assessment*, London: NUT.

Six Unions (1993), *A Framework for Reviewing the National Curriculum*, London: NUT.

Watkins, P. (1993), 'The National Curriculum – An Agenda for the Nineties', in Chitty, C. and Simon, B. (eds), *Education Answers Back: Critical Responses to Government Policy*, London: Lawrence and Wishart.

Webb, Rita (1994), 'On a Mission to Marsham Street', in *Local Government Chronicle*, 28 October.

Webb, Rosemary (1993), *Eating the Elephant Bit by Bit: The National Curriculum at Key Stage 2*, London: ATL.

Webb, Rosemary (1994), *After the Deluge: Changing Roles and Responsibilities in the Primary School*, London: ATL.

Woodhead, C. (1995), *RSA Annual Lecture*, London: RSA.

Appendix I
Interim Dearing Report
July 1993
Report Summary

The National Curriculum and the ten-level scale

1.1   The National Curriculum of ten subjects has wide support. Together with religious education, it has provided breadth and
depth to education and is now widely regarded as an entitlement
for all pupils. The Office for Standards in Education has advised
that it is beginning to raise standards, most noticeably in primary
schools.

1.2   The need for higher standards of achievement is clear from international comparisons, from recent reports such as that of the
Adult Literacy and Basic Skills Unit, and from the concerns which
continue to be expressed by employers. Under-achievement
threatens national standards of living and bears directly on the
kind of jobs and, indeed, the prospect of worthwhile employment,
of our future adult population. It undermines the potential quality of life for the individual and for society as a whole.

1.3   It is reassuring, therefore, that the reforms of the *Education Reform
Act 1988* are raising national educational standards. But the
conclusion in this Report is that we have much to learn from the
problems teachers have experienced in administering the reforms.
We can do a better job. In responding to these problems, however,
we must not cast aside what is good. We need to recognise that a
major element in teachers' present concern about workload arises
from the attempt to respond to all the changes (not just those
necessitated by the National Curriculum and its assessment) that
have been taking place, and from the pace at which change has
been sought. We need to remember, moreover, that the classroom
teacher in primary schools has faced a very considerable challenge
as each National Curriculum Order has been introduced. As time
moves on, and the Orders become more familiar, the pressures
will, to some extent, ease.

1.4   The problem of curriculum overload stems, in part, from the fact that the original Working Groups established to define the content of each Order were not able to judge the collective weight in teaching terms of the curriculum as a whole. Neither was it possible to avoid some overlap of content between subjects. A further problem stems from the fact that the attempt to spell out the requirements of each National Curriculum subject in a clear, unambiguous manner has led to a level of prescription that many teachers find unacceptably constricting. The balance between what is defined nationally and what is left to the exercise of professional judgement needs to be reviewed.

1.5   There was an admirable concern, in devising the present arrangements, that parents, pupils and teachers should have a reliable and nationally uniform measure of a pupil's progress throughout his/her school years. This has been sought through the creation of a ten-level scale for most subjects, each step of which is identified in detail through the definition of the knowledge, understanding and skills which must be mastered at each level. The aim has been to rank knowledge and skills hierarchically, level by level, from the age of 5 through to 16. This was a bold initiative and a decision on its future needs care and further consultation.

1.6   That decision is, however, needed before individual subject Orders can be revised. Certainly the scale of the administration involved in recording progress through the various statements of attainment has been daunting; it has been a significant factor in workload difficulties. The ten-level scale itself has, moreover, given rise to many problems. It is essential that we address these problems and find ways of reducing the administrative burden.

1.7   Against this background, section 3 of this Interim Report makes the following recommendations.

    (i)   Each National Curriculum Order should be revised to divide existing content into a statutory core which must be taught and optional studies which can be covered at the discretion of the individual teacher. The central importance of the core subjects of English, mathematics and science means that the statutory core in these subjects will be larger than that of the other subjects.

    (ii)   The number of statements of attainment on which teachers are currently required to make judgements should be greatly reduced. This would allow teachers to exercise their professional judgement as to whether, in the round, the pupil's knowledge, skills and understanding match assessment objectives for the relevant level.

(iii) This restructuring should take place within a clear policy framework for each key stage which identifies an appropriate margin of time for the teacher to use as he/she sees fit in the light of local circumstance.

(iv) These margins should range from 10–15% to 20–25% of teaching time, after the requirements of the National Curriculum and religious education have been met, with the smallest margin being for the 5–7 year olds where mastery of the core subjects and, in particular, the basic skills is fundamental to everything that follows at school.

(v) These margins should be used at the discretion of the school to teach optional content outside the statutory core of each National Curriculum Order and/or to introduce, for example, a foreign language at the primary stage where the school has the necessary expertise.

(vi) As has recently been announced for technology, changes in the English Order should be postponed so as to allow the revised Order for these subjects to reflect the recommendations emerging from the present Review.

(vii) The National Curriculum should continue to be available to pupils with special educational needs. Appropriate ways of recognizing progress should be found which are based on realistic expectations of what those with severe learning difficulties can achieve.

1.8   Three major issues are identified in sections 3 and 4 for consultation in the second stage of the Review.

(i) Should the ten-level scale be modified to make it more effective or should a new approach to the assessment of pupil progress be developed, which, while retaining a significant element of criterion-referencing, abandons the attempt to measure achievement from 5–16 on any single scale?

(ii) Is the revision of the ten National Curriculum subjects best undertaken through a simultaneous review of each subject, through a two-stage review based on a clear statement of guiding principles, or, as assumed in the remit, through a rolling review which occupies, say, five years?

(iii) Should there be a modified approach to the curriculum from 14–16 to provide a smoother transition to study post-16 and to respond sensitively to the developing needs of all our young people?

1.9   The strengths and weaknesses of these options must be examined very carefully before any decisions are reached. We must be confident that the changes which eventually emerge can be managed in the classroom and by the newly created School Curriculum and Assessment Authority. One of the lessons to be learned from the past is that of misjudging the manageability of change.

1.10   The third of the issues referred to in paragraph 1.8 was not within my remit but arose repeatedly during the Review. Most students now continue in some form of education and training post-16 and we need to think through pathways from 14 to 19 and beyond. It is clear that many people support the idea that change is needed, but, as yet, beyond the recognition that students should be able to follow courses that develop their particular talents, there is no consensus as to what that change should be. Section 3 of the Report, therefore, proposes further consultation on this matter of broad educational policy.

The national tests and teacher assessment

1.11   National tests have been a matter of public controversy throughout this Review. There have, in particular, been strong representations from teachers and their associations about the use of national tests for performance tables. The use of such tables lies outside the scope of this Review. But the balance between teacher assessment and national tests, and the respective purposes of each, are central to it.

1.12   It is particularly important that we are clear about the purposes of national tests as distinct from those of teacher assessment.

1.13   Teacher assessment lies at the heart of the learning progress in that new learning must be matched to what a pupil already knows and can do. It is the teacher in his/her classroom who, day in day out, undertakes this vitally important task of formative assessment.

1.14   Properly moderated teacher assessment can also contribute important summative information about a pupil's achievements. The standard national tests, however, have a key role to play here. They provide a reliable means of establishing levels of achievement by pupils in schools throughout the country. In addition they contribute to the moderation of teacher assessment and provide hard information upon which a school can make judgements about the targeting of resources and the definition of in-service training priorities. They also, as the Office for Standards in Education has reported, play an important part in raising professional expectation about what pupils can achieve. Given that the National Curriculum was introduced to raise standards, this is a major point.

1.15   Section 5 of the Report concludes, therefore, that the purpose of national tests is primarily to provide a summative contribution to the assessment of performance. Any diagnostic or formative elements should be subsidiary to that purpose and only exceptionally included if they are shown, by careful analysis, to be a cost-effective way of contributing to the formative information a teacher needs about his/her pupils.

1.16   The Secretary of State for Education accepted recommendations made at an early stage in the Review that the mandatory national tests in 1994 should be limited to the core subjects and that they should cover only Key Stage 1 (pupils aged 7) and Key Stage 3 (pupils aged 14). He also decided, and announced in Parliament at the same time, that there should be some substantial streamlining of the tests. The advice of the School Examinations and Assessment Council, which is set out in detail in section 5 and annex 6, is summarised in paragraph 1.17 below.

1.17   At Key Stage 1, the Report recommends that in 1994 science should be covered by statutory teacher assessment and the pupil time required for English and mathematics tests should be reduced by between 25% and 50% depending on the attainment of the pupil. In Key Stage 3, the Report recommends that the pupil time required for national tests in England should be reduced from a total of 12½ hours in 1993 to 6¾ hours. Voluntary national pilots in the core subjects are recommended for Key Stage 2.

1.18   I recommend (section 5) giving equal standing to teacher assessment and to national tests in reporting to parents and others by whatever means.

1.19   I make suggestions in section 5 on the balance between teacher assessment and national tests in the medium term. I also recommend that:

(i) with the possible exception set out in paragraph 1.20 below, national testing should be limited for the next three years to the core subjects of English, mathematics and science in Key Stages 1, 2 and 3;

(ii) the School Curriculum and Assessment Authority should accordingly give priority to providing high quality standard tests in the core subjects.

1.20   For 1996 at the end of Key Stage 3, consideration might be given to national tests in those subjects which pupils will cease to study after that age so that there is a definitive entry of attainment in the student's Record of Achievement.

1.21   Recommendations on the form of teacher assessment for the medium term for the non-core foundation subjects will be made in the Final Report.

Effective administration

1.22   The final element in my remit related to improving the administration of the National Curriculum and assessment. Section 6 of the Report contains many specific recommendations since the issues here relate to detail rather than to policy. The recommendations cover arrangements for providing earlier decisions; for simplification and greater clarity; for better distribution arrangements; and for the provision of better and earlier information to schools to allow proper time for planning.

The underlying concern

1.23   The underlying concern of the Report is to lift educational standards. I recommend that the curricular and administrative complexity must be reduced and the excessive prescription of the National Curriculum removed particularly outside the core subjects. This is a recognition that the professionalism of teachers must be trusted. Trust carries with it, however, the duty of accountability: the greater the trust, the clearer the accountability must be.

Other issues

1.24 The Report makes two recommendations for research projects:

(i) in collaboration with the Office for Standards in Education, the development of an approach to the assessment of the value added by schools (section 4 and annex 5);

(ii) in collaboration with the Office for Standards in Education and the Department for Education, the development of approaches to quality assurance in schools which might lead to the accreditation of schools for assessment purposes (section 5 and annex 7).

Next steps

1.25 A Final Report is required by the end of the year. That provides time for wider consultation on the major issues of curriculum structure and the approach to its revision outlined in this Report.

1.26 Meanwhile, as recommended in section 7, preliminary work should begin on the approach to slimming down the curriculum and on reducing greatly the present statements of attainment.

Appendix II
Final Dearing Report
December 1993

2.1   The National Curriculum is fundamental to raising educational standards. Urgent action is needed to reduce the statutorily required content of its programmes of study and to make it less prescriptive and less complex. A closely co-ordinated review of all the statutory curriculum Orders should immediately be put in hand, guided by the need to:

(i)   reduce the volume of material required by law to be taught;

(ii) simplify and clarify the programmes of study;

(iii) reduce prescription so as to give more scope for professional judgement;

(iv) ensure that the Orders are written in a way which offers maximum support to the classroom teacher.

Paragraph 3.8

Slimming the curriculum at Key Stages 1, 2 and 3

2.2   The primary purpose of the review at Key Stages 1, 2 and 3 should be to slim down the National Curriculum; to make the Orders less prescriptive; and to free some 20% of teaching time for use at the discretion of the school.

Paragraphs 4.16 and 4.29

2.3   The review should, therefore, be primarily concerned with dividing the content of the present curriculum Orders between a statutory core and optional material for use at the discretion of the school. The slimming down should take place in the context of curricular objectives for each key stage with all Orders being revised together.

Paragraphs 4.3–4.4

2.4   The first priority for discretionary time must be to support work in the basics of literacy, oracy and numeracy. Beyond this, the bulk of the time released should be used for work in those National Curriculum subjects which the school chooses to explore in more depth. In addition to the National Curriculum subjects and religious education, time must also be found at Key Stage 3 for sex education as required by law and for careers education and guidance.

Paragraphs 3.26, 4.46 and 4.47

2.5   Schools should be accountable to their governing bodies for using the time released effectively. The school's decisions should be recorded and available for inspection.

Paragraph 4.48

2.6   The review should define the essential matters, skills and processes which must be taught at each key stage and should not change the basic content of the programmes of study except where there is a clear need to do so. The more radically the Orders are changed, the greater the time schools will need to plan for their introduction.

Paragraphs 3.26, 4.33 and 8.4

2.7   The opportunity should, however, be taken to reduce the present numbers of attainment targets and statements of attainment. The scope for reducing the number of attainment targets is greatest at the lower levels. The aim in reducing the number of statements of attainment should be to produce a definition of what is expected at each level which is sufficiently clear and rigorous to be of use to teachers, but which avoids the excessive detail of the current approach.

Paragraphs 4.3vii, 4.45 and 7.29

2.8   The National Curriculum Council's (NCC) recommendations for revised attainment targets and programmes of study for English and design & technology should provide the basis for the review of these subjects. Pending the introduction of a new design & technology curriculum, schools should be able to make applications under section 16 of the Education Reform Act 1988 to teach the curriculum proposed by the NCC on an experimental basis in Key Stages 1, 2 and 3.

Paragraphs 4.36–4.37

2.9   Each National Curriculum subject should continue to be taught in the first three key stages, but the review should recognise the prime importance of mastery of the basics of learning at the primary stage, including literacy, oracy, numeracy and a basic competence in the use of information technology.

Paragraphs 4.5–4.7

2.10   The revised Orders should be presented in single volumes for Key Stages I and 2.

Paragraph 4.35

2.11   The review should be undertaken by the School Curriculum and Assessment Authority (SCAA) whose senior officers should be assisted by advisory groups for each key stage and subject. Their membership should include teachers and headteachers (primary and secondary). The SCAA should work closely with the Curriculum Council for Wales in this review, particularly in subjects for which the curriculum is common to England and Wales.

Paragraphs 4.49–4.53 and Appendix 5

2.12   Final decisions on the balance of statutory provision for the subjects should be taken in the light of advice from groups set up by the School Curriculum and Assessment Authority. To assist the groups in this task, the Report offers guidance on the time which should be assumed to be available for each subject at each key stage. A major reduction will be required in the content of the non-core subjects at Key Stages 1 and 2.

Paragraphs 4.20–4.32

2.13   No further major changes should be made to the National Curriculum Orders for five years following the review.

Paragraph 4.54

Revising the curriculum at Key Stage 4

2.14   At Key Stage 4, schools should have greater opportunity to offer a curriculum which meets the distinctive talents and individual aspirations of their students. The mandatory requirements should be limited to English, mathematics and single science, physical education and short courses in a modern foreign language and technology. Religious education and sex education must, in addition, be taught by law. Careers education is also particularly important at this key stage. These minimum requirements will allow greater scope for academic and vocational options.

Paragraphs 5.17–5.26

2.15   As an objective for the medium term, a General National Vocational Qualification (GNVQ) option should be developed for use at Key Stage 4 as part of a wider curriculum. But its general introduction must be dependent upon the development of courses and assessments of the highest quality. Meanwhile, the School Curriculum and Assessment Authority (SCAA) should discuss with the National Council for Vocational Qualifications (NCVQ) whether and how work undertaken as part of GCSE courses could count towards GNVQ accreditation. The SCAA should continue, in particular, to discuss with the NCVQ the possibility of a 'Part One' qualification for the foundation and intermediate levels of the GNVQ.

Paragraphs 5.31–5.39 and 5.42–5.43

2.16   Further thought should be given to the introduction of a National Vocational Qualification option as part of a wider curriculum at Key Stage 4.

Paragraph 5.40

2.17   The present requirement for National Curriculum short courses to be combined with another short course for accreditation purposes should be abandoned. Urgent attention should be given as to how free-standing short courses might best be accredited.

Paragraph 5.44

2.18   The School Curriculum and Assessment Authority should consult the GCSE examining boards on whether the scope for offering somewhat different syllabuses in the GCSE examinations should be enlarged by reducing the content of the National Curriculum subjects which is statutorily prescribed.

Paragraph 5.47

2.19   The recommendation that history and geography should no longer be mandatory subjects in Key Stage 4 should take immediate effect to avoid uncertainty in schools, examining bodies and publishers.

Paragraph 5.49

2.20   Pending the introduction of a revised Order for technology in 1996 at Key Stage 4 (1995 for Key Stages 1, 2 and 3), this subject should not be compulsory for students entering Key Stage 4 in 1994 and 1995.

Paragraph 5.50

Accountability and reporting

2.21   The increased trust placed in schools and teachers by reducing prescription in the curriculum and freeing up time for use at their own discretion should be complemented by proper accountability to parents and more widely through the provision of information, including that from simple, national tests in the core subjects, about progress and achievement.

Paragraphs 3.34–3.40

2.22   The School Curriculum and Assessment Authority should accept full accountability for its performance and publish an annual report to the Secretary of State for Education reporting on its work, good and bad.

Paragraphs 3.41–3.43

Special educational needs

2.23   The National Curriculum should be available to pupils with special educational needs.

Paragraph 6.4i

2.24   The National Curriculum levels defined in the Orders should be broadened to include level I at Key Stage 2 and levels I and 2 at Key Stage 3 to ensure that teachers can provide work wholly in line with their pupils' abilities and needs.

Paragraph 6.4ii

2.25   The work on the revision of the National Curriculum should involve teachers of all pupils with special educational needs.

Paragraph 6.4iii

2.26   Schools should liaise with parents over the development of the appropriate curriculum for statemented pupils.

Paragraph 6.5

2.27   The assessment and recording of the achievements of pupils with special educational needs (including the provision of non-statutory test material) should be reviewed by the School Curriculum and Assessment Authority (SCAA). As a first step, the SCAA should commission a study of previous work in this area by schools, local education authorities and other agencies with a view to providing guidance material for general use.

Paragraphs 6.8 and 9.15

The ten-level scale

2.28   The ten-level scale is unnecessarily complex and excessively prescriptive. It suffers from duplication and inconsistencies. These failings explain some very real problems teachers have experienced in implementing the National Curriculum.

Paragraphs 7.15–7.25

Index

A-level examinations 14, 107
accountability 19–20, 36–7, 53, 70,
    130, 133, 136
Adult Literacy and Basic Skills Unit
    (ALBSU) 125
Aldrich, R. 90
art education 39, 41–2
assessment 13, 29, 37–9, 45, 49, 53,
    68, 82–3, 91, 96–8, 136
    see also Standard Assessment Tasks
    (SATs); testing/tests
Assistant Masters' and Mistresses'
    Association 94, 114–15
Association of Teachers and Lecturers
    (ATL) 45, 59, 61–2, 103–4
Auld, R. 19–20

Bachrach, P. 105
back to basics 27–8, 31–2
Baker, K. 27, 29, 32–6, 48–51, 53,
    55–6, 72, 89–90, 93, 100
Ball, S. 14, 29
Baratz, M. 105
Barber, M. 16–17, 44, 68–71, 110–11
basic skills 21, 23
Black, E. 113
Black, P. 39, 53, 89, 93, 97–8
Black Papers 19, 22
Blair, T. 72
Blatch, E. 61, 68, 71, 97
Blunkett, D. 72
Board of Education 11, 24
Bolton, E. 89, 103
Brent Local Education Authority 30
Brighouse, T. 71
Burnham Committee 27
Butler, R. A. 15–17

Caines, J. 101
Callaghan, J. 20–4, 25, 28, 34, 90
Campbell, R. 89, 94, 113–16, 119
Cane, B. 115
careers education 133
centralization 15, 18, 25–7, 29, 74,
    85, 90
Centre for Policy Studies (CPS) 28, 51
child-centred curriculum see
    progressive tradition
Chitty, C. 90
Churchill, W. 15–16
citizenship education 16
city technology colleges 29, 109
civil servants 24–6, 38, 40–1, 43,
    49–53, 57, 86, 88, 90, 95,
    102, 119
Clarke, K. 33–4, 49, 54, 57, 100
comprehensive education/schools 21
Coopers and Lybrand 45, 101, 113
core curriculum vs. broad-based
    curriculum 25, 32, 35–6, 39,
    63, 90
council tax 30
Cove, W. G. 17
Cox, B. 56–7, 78
Crosland, A. 100
cultural-analysis tradition 14
cultural-restorationists 27–8, 31, 35
curriculum continuity 36, 74
curriculum development 9–15, 17–18,
    25–6
    see also National Curriculum
curriculum models see specific
    models, e.g. liberal-humanist
    tradition
curriculum study group 18, 25

Dainton, S. 43, 45, 51, 59, 61–2, 111
Dearing, R. 51, 61–2, 65–6, 68, 101, 103–7, 112
Dearing Reports/Reviews 11, 47, 62–5, 67–70, 72, 80, 104, Appendices 1 and 2
de Caux, A. 111
decentralization 18–19, 21, 26–7, 72, 74, 82
Department for Education 51, 61, 80, 100–1
   Choice and Diversity: A New Framework for Schools 99, 102, 110
Department for Education and Employment 28, 51, 101, 103, 108
Department of Education and Science 28, 34, 38, 40–3, 48–9, 90, 100–1, 103
   Better schools 26, 90
   'Children and their primary schools. Vol. 1. The Report' (The Plowden Report) 12, 19
   Circular 14/77 25
   Circular 5/89 92
   'Education in schools: A Consultative Documents' (cmnd 6869) 25
   'National Curriculum: From Policy to Practice' 40–2, 96
   'The National Curriculum 5–16: A Consultation Document' 36
   Task Group on Assessment and Testing, report 93, 98
   Task Group on Assessment and Testing, three supplementary reports 93
Department of Trade and Industry (DTI) 28
design education 41, 133
Dewey, J. 12, 14
Dorrance, R. 101

economic education relationship 18–19, 21, 30
Education Act (1944) 16–17
Education Act (1988) 17, 27–9, 39–40, 76, 87, 90–1, 99, 102, 118–19, 125, 133

Education Act (1992) 87
Education Reform Bill 39, 91, 95
education vouchers 28–9
educational finance 23–4, 28–9, 120
educational objectives 12, 17, 23, 31–2, 35–6, 75
Ellis, T. 19–20
English studies 31, 41–2, 48, 51–3, 55–60, 78–9, 83–4, 92, 98, 110–11, 118, 127, 129–30, 134
Evans, A. 26, 43

5–14 curriculum 65
14–19 curriculum 65, 85, 113
France 55–6
Funding Agency for Schools (FAS) 102–3
Further and Higher Education Act (1992) 102

General Certificate of Secondary Education (GCSE) 13–14, 37, 43, 57, 65, 107–8, 135
General National Vocational Qualifications (GNVQ) 97, 108, 135
geography 41, 135
girls' education *see* women's education
Girls' School Association 109
Golby, M. 10, 14
Gould, R. 18, 21, 25–6
Graham, D. 40, 43, 48–51, 57, 89, 92, 94, 98–9, 101, 114–15
grammar schools 11
grant-maintained schools 29, 32, 52, 86, 102
Griffiths, B. 51, 58, 65, 101

Hall, J. 111
Halsey, P. 40, 51, 101
Hancock, D. 101
Hargreaves, D. 99
Haringey Local Education Authority 30
Haviland, J. 95
Headmasters' Conference 109
Heath, E. 18–19

Her Majesty's Inspectors (HMI) 41–2, 49
'Aspects of Secondary Education in England' 25
Hewton, E. 44
hidden curriculum 10
Higher Education Funding Council (HEFC) 102
Hilditch, B. 110–11
Hilsum, S. 114
history 41, 48–9, 77–8, 118, 135
Holland, G. 61, 68, 71, 101
home economics 16–17, 37
Howarth, A. 118

Independent Association of Preparatory Schools 109
independent schools 11, 16, 29, 108–9
industrial-modernizers 28, 31, 35
industry–education relationship 21–2, 23, 28, 31
information technology 28, 63, 96, 107, 134
Inner London Education Authority 19–20
Iven, H. 111

Joseph, K. 25–9, 34, 95

Key Stage 1 42, 45, 47, 54–5, 63, 77, 80, 83–4, 91, 96, 98, 106, 108, 114–15, 129–30, 132–4, 136
Key Stage 2 42, 46–7, 63, 77, 80, 83–4, 91, 96, 98, 102, 106, 108, 113, 130, 132–4, 136
Key Stage 3 47, 54–5, 57, 61, 77, 80, 83–4, 91, 96, 98, 107–8, 129–30, 132–3, 136
Key Stage 4 42, 47, 68, 77, 91, 96, 108, 134–5
Kingman, J. 56
Kogan, M. 100

Labour government/Party 16, 19–25, 30–2, 72–3
Lancaster, T. 101
Lawlor, S. 29
Lawton, D. 14

league tables 29, 53, 69, 71–2, 84–6, 98, 108
Leeds University 54
Lennon, J. 13
liberal-humanist tradition 10–11, 13–14, 28
Liverpool Local Education Authority 30
local education authorities 17–18, 25, 29–30, 41–2, 46, 86, 103
see also specific local education authorities, e.g. Brent Local Education Authority
local management of schools 29, 42, 86
Logan, D. G. 17
London Association for the Teaching of English (LATE) 58

McAvoy, D. 59, 71
MacGregor, J. 57, 95, 100
Maclure, S. 90
Major, J. 28, 57, 71
Manpower Services Commission (MSC) 28
Marenbon, J. 89, 95
market forces 28–9, 32, 89
mathematics education 22, 31, 39, 41–2, 57, 83–4, 91, 94, 129–30, 134
Miller, J. 111
modern language studies 41, 96, 127
Moore, T. 16–17
moral development/education 31, 99
music education 39, 41–2

National Association for the Teaching of English (NATE) 58, 79, 83
National Association of Head Teachers (NAHT) 45, 84
National Association of Schoolmasters Union of Women Teachers (NASUWT) 60–2, 103–4, 113
National Association of Teachers in Further and Higher Education (NATFHE) 112

National Council for Vocational
  Qualifications (NCVQ) 14, 103,
  108, 135
National Curriculum
  attainment targets 37–8, 41, 91,
    96, 107, 126–7, 133, 136
  consultation process 37–8, 41, 43,
    48, 64–7, 94, 106–7, 109–13,
    118, 134
  core subjects 36–7, 91–2, 94–6,
    106, 130
  cross-curricular approach 50, 77,
    96–8, 113
  design of 35–8, 80–2, 90–2, 94–5,
    96–9, 105
  development of 34, 40–2, 45–50,
    55–7, 62–5, 68–9, 72–3, 75–9,
    92–4, 106, 120, 125–8, 130–1,
    Appendix 2
  draft Orders 41, 48–9
  evaluation of 45, 49, 52, 54,
    113–17
  foundation subjects 36–7, 40–1,
    91–2, 96, 99, 105, 107, 125
  implementation of 39–42, 48, 63,
    68, 93–5
  non-statutory working groups 41,
    56, 92, 94
  objectives 29–31, 34–6, 74–5,
    90–1
  origins 15–27, 33–42, 92–3
  policy development within 34,
    44–5, 50, 65–8, 72, 80, 88–120
  programmes of study 38, 41, 69,
    77, 82–3, 91, 94, 132
  review/revision of 61–4, 68, 72,
    74, 78, 80–2, 97, 110, 112
    see also Dearing Reports/Reviews
  secrecy about 34, 51–2
  separate subject teaching 77
  statutory Orders 41, 51–2, 57,
    68–9, 72, 76, 78, 81–3, 91, 107,
    110–12, 117–18, 126, 132–4, 136
    see also specific curriculum
    subjects, e.g. English studies
National Curriculum Council (NCC)
  40, 42–3, 46–7, 49–52, 61–4, 66,
  78, 80, 92, 94–5, 99, 101, 103,
  106, 109–11, 133

*Curriculum Guidance 3: The Whole
  Curriculum* 96
'The National Curriculum: An
  Overview of the Cross-Curricular
  Themes' 97
'Spiritual and Moral
  Development: A Discussion
  Paper' 99
National Union of Elementary
  Teachers (NUET) 16
National Union of Teachers (NUT)
  16–18, 25–6, 43, 45–6, 54, 58–60,
  62, 71–3, 79, 104, 111
  'Miss, the Rabbit Ate the Floating
  Apple: An Evaluation of the KS1
  Tests' 54
Neill, S. 94, 113–16
Nicolle, H. 66, 101
Northern Ireland 108

Office for Standards in Education
  (OFSTED) 49, 83, 86, 101–2,
  113, 125, 131
O'Hear, P. 75
open enrolment 29, 32
Osborne, M. 113

parent choice 85
Pascall, D. 51–2, 61, 63, 92, 97–9,
  101, 110
Patten, J. 52–3, 58–9, 61–2, 65, 68,
  71, 100, 102–4
payment by results 15–16
physical education 41–2
Plaskow, M. 18
Plowden Report *see* Department of
  Education and Science, 'Children
  and their primary schools. Vol. 1.
  The Report'
poll tax 30
Pollard, A. 90
Popper, K. 94
primary curriculum/education/
  teachers 12, 76–7, 96, 114–15,
  117, 125, 134
  see also Key Stages 1 and 2
progressive tradition 11–13, 19
public expenditure 30
  see also educational finance

public schools *see* independent
   schools
pupil evaluation 82–3

Raban, B. 52, 110
records of achievement 130
religious education 37, 90, 92, 107,
   115, 125, 134
revised codes of education 15
Ridley, N. 28
Rousseau, J. J. 12
Ruddock, J. 18
Rumbold, A. 91

Sayer, J. 89
School Curriculum and Assessment
   Authority (SCAA) 14, 61, 64,
   66–8, 80–1, 84, 99, 101–3, 105,
   107–10, 112–13, 116–19, 128,
   134–6
   *National Curriculum Subject
   Draft Proposals and Overview
   Document* 97
   *Religious Education: Model Syllabus –
   The Legal Requirement* 90
School Curriculum Development
   Committee (SCDC) 26, 40, 44
school day 91–2, 106–8, 127
school effectiveness 73
School Examination and Assessment
   Council (SEAC) 40, 42–3, 46,
   49, 51, 54, 59–60, 92, 101, 106,
   109, 129
school governors/school governing
   bodies 41–2, 133
school improvement 73
School Teachers' Pay and Conditions
   Act (1991) 102
School Teachers' Review Body
   102–3, 116
Schools' Council 18, 25–6, 40, 42, 44
science education 21, 28, 39, 41–3,
   57, 74, 83, 91, 94, 129–30, 134
Scotland 108
Secondary Examinations Council
   (SEC) 26, 40, 44
Secondary Heads' Association 110
secondary school teachers 115–16
sex education 133–4

Shephard, G. 71, 100, 102, 107
Shorrocks, D. 113
special educational needs 127, 136
Standard Assessment Tasks (SATs)
   40, 45–6, 54, 91, 93
   see also testing/tests
standards 20–3, 31, 34, 36, 39, 47,
   67–70, 72, 75, 85, 89, 94, 115,
   118, 125, 129, 132
Sutherland, S. 101

Task Group on Assessment and
   Testing (TGAT) 38, 53, 93,
   97–8
Tate, N. 105
Tawney, R. H. 21
teacher appraisal 42
teacher assessment 38, 53, 82–4, 98,
   126–30
teacher attitudes 19–20, 30, 34, 39,
   45–8, 54, 57, 69–70, 75, 79, 83,
   85, 95, 102, 110, 115, 120
teacher education 102
teacher expectations 75
teacher participation 18, 25–7, 41
teacher redeployment 42
Teacher Training Agency (TTA) 102
teacher workload 46, 54, 60, 68–9,
   71, 82, 84, 89, 98, 103–4, 107–8,
   112–16, 125–6
teachers' associations/unions 16,
   25–7, 39, 42–7, 51, 58–70, 73, 82,
   98, 106–7, 109–13, 118
   'A Framework for Reviewing the
   National Curriculum' 62–4,
   111–12
   see also specific organizations, e.g.
   National Union of Teachers
teaching profession 21–2, 26–7, 30,
   46, 72–3, 119, 130
Tebbit, N. 36
Technical and Vocational Education
   Initiative (TVEI) 14, 28
technocratic tradition 13
technology education 28, 41, 110,
   133, 135
testing/tests 38–9, 53–5, 57–62, 65,
   69, 82–3, 93, 97–8, 102, 113,
   128–30

boycotts 45, 54, 58–62, 64–5,
  67–8, 70–2, 104, 112
  external marking of 84, 98
  validity 83
  see also assessment; Standard
  Assessment Tasks (SATs)
Thatcher, M. 28, 30–2, 34–5, 37–9, 48
The Treasury, *Economic Appraisal in
  Central Government: a Technical
  Guide for Government
  Departments.* 119
Tytler, D. 89, 92

urban education/schools 12, 31

vouchers *see* education vouchers

Wales 108
Wandsworth Local Education
  Authority 60, 62
Warwick University 45, 52, 110,
  114–16
Watkins, P. 93
Webb, Rita 88
Webb, Rosemary 89, 108, 113, 117
White, J. 75
whole curriculum, the 96–8
William Tyndale School 12, 19, 22,
  30, 44
women's education 16–17, 21
Wood, R. S. 24
Woodhead, C. 12, 52, 64, 66, 68, 99,
  101, 106, 111